T0334116

Cambridge Elements ⹇

Elements in Semantics
edited by
Jonathan Ginzburg
Université Paris-Cité
Daniel Lassiter
University of Edinburgh

SEMANTICS AND DEEP LEARNING

Lasha Abzianidze
Utrecht University

Lisa Bylinina
Utrecht University

Denis Paperno
Utrecht University

CAMBRIDGE
UNIVERSITY PRESS

Shaftesbury Road, Cambridge CB2 8EA, United Kingdom

One Liberty Plaza, 20th Floor, New York, NY 10006, USA

477 Williamstown Road, Port Melbourne, VIC 3207, Australia

314–321, 3rd Floor, Plot 3, Splendor Forum, Jasola District Centre,
New Delhi – 110025, India

103 Penang Road, #05–06/07, Visioncrest Commercial, Singapore 238467

Cambridge University Press is part of Cambridge University Press & Assessment,
a department of the University of Cambridge.

We share the University's mission to contribute to society through the pursuit of
education, learning and research at the highest international levels of excellence.

www.cambridge.org
Information on this title: www.cambridge.org/9781009542395

DOI: 10.1017/9781009542340

When citing this work, please include a reference to the DOI 10.1017/9781009542340

First published 2024

A catalogue record for this publication is available from the British Library.

ISBN 978-1-009-54239-5 Hardback
ISBN 978-1-009-54236-4 Paperback
ISSN 2754-0367 (online)
ISSN 2754-0359 (print)

Semantics and Deep Learning

Elements in Semantics

DOI: 10.1017/9781009542340
First published online: December 2024

Lasha Abzianidze
Utrecht University
Lisa Bylinina
Utrecht University
Denis Paperno
Utrecht University

Author for correspondence: Lasha Abzianidze, l.abzianidze@uu.nl

Abstract: This Element covers the interaction of two research areas: linguistic semantics and deep learning. It focuses on three phenomena central to natural language interpretation: reasoning and inference, compositionality, and extralinguistic grounding. Representation of these phenomena in recent neural models is discussed, along with the quality of these representations and ways to evaluate them (datasets, tests, measures). The Element closes with suggestions on possible deeper interactions between theoretical semantics and language technology based on deep learning models.

Keywords: compositionality, grounding, inference, deep learning, large language models

ISBNs: 9781009542395 (HB) 9781009542364 (PB) 9781009542340 (OC)
ISSNs: 2754-0367 (online), 2754-0359 (print)

Contents

1 Introduction*

This Element covers the interaction of two areas of research: linguistic semantics and deep learning. These fields share a lot of mutually relevant ground, but at the same time, the dialogue between the respective research communities is often constrained by the lack of transparency in terminology and background assumptions. With this Element, we aim to foster the connections between the two fields by highlighting the relevance of these fields to each other and by providing an introduction into the points where natural language semantics and deep learning meet. Instead of enumerating all possibly relevant topics, we will take a close look at three fundamental meaning-related phenomena – semantic inference, compositionality, and extralinguistic grounding – and use them as study cases, discussing how these phenomena are treated in modern computational models. The discussion is accompanied by demonstrations that readers are invited to play with. No prior programming experience is required to run the code.[1]

In recent years, the deep learning revolution has changed the landscape of natural language processing (NLP), especially so after a deep neural architecture that is the basis of practically all of today's most successful models – the Transformer (Vaswani et al., 2017) – was introduced, and various models based on this architecture were trained on large quantities of primarily linguistic data. Artificial intelligence (AI) systems built on these models are growing and getting higher and higher scores on various tasks as we speak, advancing the state of the art (SOTA). These systems and tools are rapidly becoming a part of everyday life for more and more people, obviously so after the notable release of one such system, ChatGPT, in late 2022.[2]

Given the ever-growing omnipresence of such tools, a solid understanding of both their successes and weaknesses is important. Some of the seemingly simple but at the same time fundamental questions that one can ask here are: Do these models *understand* the texts they process and produce? Do they capture the *meaning* of texts in natural language?

There are two aspects to these questions: an instrumental and a theoretical one. Instrumentally, the answer depends on how well deep learning models perform on tasks that – presumably – require semantic competence. As the discussion that follows will show, despite the fact that deep learning models

---

* The authors are listed in alphabetical order. Given the authors' equal contribution, each author has a right to list themselves as a first author when citing this Element. Main author of Section 2 "Textual Inference": Lasha Abzianidze; main author of Section 3 "Compositionality": Denis Paperno; main author of Section 4 "Grounding: Language and Vision": Lisa Bylinina. Introduction and Conclusions: equal contribution.

[1] See our public repository at https://github.com/kovvalsky/SemDL for code and demos for the three phenomena discussed in this Element.

[2] https://openai.com/blog/chatgpt.

have pushed the SOTA forward in many areas of NLP, what kinds of linguistic – and in particular, semantic – knowledge these models develop as a result of training is still the subject of ongoing study. Indeed, NLP evaluation is typically organized around datasets that may or may not reflect the generality and real nature of linguistic knowledge. More specifically, various semantic tasks reportedly still prove hard for modern models despite their superficial success.

On a theoretical level, the answer to these questions obviously depends on *what meaning is* and *what is required of true natural language understanding*. These questions lie at the core of the discipline of theoretical semantics. Theoretical choices concerning the nature of linguistic meanings provide a framework for the instrumental evaluation and development of NLP systems: What do we need to test in order to address models' semantic capabilities? What types of learning agents do we think lead to better meaning representations?

This instrumental–theoretical relation goes both ways: On the one hand, theories of how humans convey and extract linguistic meanings set the stage for what to expect from artificial linguistic systems and agents. On the other hand, performance of deep learning models can inform linguistic theory: If we observe a particular success or failure of a model on some task, is it expected under our view on how meanings are represented and acquired, given how this model was trained? Or should we adjust our theoretical understanding of semantics accordingly?

These are all questions with no definitive answers, and we will not try to pretend otherwise in this Element. Instead, we will give substance to the debates around these questions and invite the readers to think about them together with us.

We start with laying out the necessary technical background on text representation in models of interest. Then we establish the theoretical context for our discussion and how it relates to the current debates about semantics in such models.

Then we move on to the three topics this Element will focus on. We start from the *inferential* perspective on semantics in Section 2. We discuss how deep learning systems apply to modeling inference between sentences or larger linguistic units. Then, in Section 3, we discuss how vector-based and deep learning methods approach the phenomenon of semantic compositionality, and how semantic compositionality is tested and probed. Finally, in Section 4, we turn to the quickly developing field of language and vision, where *referential* properties of language expressions receive an automated treatment. We discuss the representation of these phenomena in recent neural models and the quality of these representations, as well as ways to evaluate them. We close the Element with directions for future research and deeper possible interconnections between deep learning and theoretical semantics.

1.1 Technical Context: Vector Representations

Artificial neural networks are mathematical structures that formalize data processing as operations over numeric vectors. Let us unpack this.

Word Vectors   A (k-dimensional) vector is a sequence of k numbers. Vectors or vector combinations can represent diverse kinds of data, including linguistic data. For example, one version of GloVe (Pennington, Socher & Manning, 2014) assigns every word of English a fifty-dimensional vector:

$$\text{to: } \langle 0.680, -0.039, \quad 0.302, \ldots, -0.073, -0.065, -0.260 \rangle$$

$$\text{and: } \langle 0.268, \quad 0.143, -0.279, \ldots, -0.632, -0.250, -0.381 \rangle$$

$$\text{government: } \langle 0.388, -1.083, \quad 0.450, \ldots, 1.194, -0.653, -0.763 \rangle.$$

Vectors in GloVe and other models are estimated from data, most commonly from the way words are used in texts. The numeric values in resulting word vectors encode diverse word properties correlated with word usage, including semantic and syntactic properties. Simplifying, one can think of these values as encoding word features including part of speech, gender, animacy, etcetera, although the values are continuous and do not correspond to interpretable features in a perfect or one-to-one fashion. So while the dimensions are usually estimated from distributions, they can be seen as reflecting an underlying conceptual space in the spirit of Gardenfors (2004).

Relations between word vectors are often regular, allowing for methods such as vector analogy solving: to solve *UK:London=France:?*, one can apply arithmetic operations to words involved and search for a word with the nearest vector to *vec(London)-vec(UK)+vec(France)*.

1.1.1 Word Embedding Models and Neural Language Models

Naturally occurring texts are a rich source of data. The task of language models (LMs) to predict continuation of a textual sequence can be also thought of as the task of classifying contexts (sequences of words) according to which word(s) can serve as a likely continuation of the context. In this case, the number of classes is huge as each vocabulary item is its own class.

For example, one can take as input a single word context (e.g., *scientific*), encode it as a vector, and use the model to predict likelihood scores for different words to appear in the context of *scientific*. Such a model will assign high scores to words like *approach* or *major*, and low scores to words that are not particularly likely to appear near *scientific*. In practice, a model represents each context (e.g., the word *scientific*) with a relatively low dimensional vector v from which a vector of scores for all vocabulary items is derived via matrix multiplication $M^{WE}v$, where the word embedding matrix M^{WE} contains compact vectors of words in the vocabulary. There are good reasons to use vectors of relatively low dimensionality. First, they are more practical in computation, including various vector operations used in neural network models. Second, features of lower dimensional vectors may better approximate abstract features of words, including features corresponding to semantic properties. Because of this, inputs with similarities in meaning or syntactic properties end up with substantial overlap in their vector features.

Systems that predict likely words in this way are known as word embedding models. They operate with individual word inputs, as in the example just provided.

Early methods that estimated word vectors from corpus data included the Hyperspace Analog of Language (Burgess & Lund, 1995) and Latent Semantic Analysis, also known as LSA (Landauer & Dumais, 1997). The advent of neural network methods in the 2010s led to the creation of several efficient algorithms for word vector estimation, which were released as word2vec (Mikolov et al., 2013) and GloVe (Pennington et al., 2014). Similar to word2vec, fastText (Bojanowski et al., 2017) extended its coverage to rare and unseen words by exploiting cues from the character sequences within the word. These algorithms proved robust and fared better in empirical evaluations than earlier methods (Baroni, Dinu, & Kruszewski, 2014).

In contrast to (static) word embedding models, *neural LMs* predict the probability distribution over the next word (or other text elements) given a sequence of other elements in context – for example, the sequence *Let's use the scientific ...* or *The cat is sitting ...*). For the latter sequence, the next word prediction may look as in Table 1. As seen in this example, the sequence is predicted to be continued with a dot or "on," with prepositions like "under" or "by" predicted less likely, and many other words having negligible predicted probabilities (rounded to 0 in Table 1).

The Sequence Neural Models: From Recurrent Networks to Transformers
Often, vector operations proceed via multiple computation steps – that is, output vector v is computed from vector u that is itself computed from the input vector x. The intermediate computation steps are called the *hidden layers* of the model, and a model that includes hidden layers is considered a *deep* neural network. Machine learning methods that create such models are known as deep learning.

Table 1 Neural word embedding models (and neural language models) assign, for a given context, an array of *logit* scores to each element of the model's vocabulary, which can then be transformed into probabilities using the softmax function.

Classes	on	the	by	.	from	he	my	at	under	...
Scores	7.1	2.3	2.6	7.5	1.8	0.22	0.25	4.74	6.0	
Probabilities	0.23	0	0.02	0.34	0	0	0	0.02	0.08	

For most purposes, assigning vectors to words is not enough if the goal is to process diverse kinds of structures, such as phrases, sentences, or longer texts. This motivates several types of sequence models, which can adapt to inputs of variable length. In all sequence models, the input is a sequence of vectors representing text units – for example, words, and the output is a sequence of calculated vectors:

$$x_1, x_2 \ldots x_n \longrightarrow h_1, h_2 \ldots h_n. \tag{1}$$

The vector representations $h_1, h_2 \ldots h_n$ that a sequence model derives can then be used for diverse tasks such as sequence classification, tagging (token classification), etcetera.

The oldest type of sequence neural network, inspired by real-time signal processing in humans, is the recurrent neural network (RNN). Recurrent neural networks process the input one element at a time, computing the memory representation h_k from h_{k-1} and the kth input element x_k. Simple recurrent networks (SRNs), proposed by Elman (1990), already showed promising results on toy linguistic input, but presented diverse problems at training time. More efficient recurrent architectures were proposed later, with two gaining wide adoption: the Long Short-Term Memory, or LSTM (Hochreiter & Schmidhuber, 1997), and the Gated Recurrent Unit, or GRU (Cho et al., 2014).

Most current applications, however, rely on the Transformer model (Vaswani et al., 2017); see Section 1.1.2. In addition to other practical benefits, the self-attention mechanism underlying Transformer models makes it easier to learn and execute nonlocal operations on the sequence.

Regardless of the precise underlying architecture, sequence models can be used to produce *contextualized token vectors*. If x_k is an input word embedding, corresponding h_k in the output represents the kth word in context. One can also select one of the output vectors, often the last one h_n, to represent the whole sequence. For example, in a task like natural language inference, the vector resulting from processing the concatenation of the premise and the hypothesis can serve to provide features labeling the example as entailment / contradiction / neutral; see Section 2.

Subword Tokenization   For practical reasons, modern NLP models limit the size of their vocabulary. As a result, neural networks often represent text as sequences of tokens, where each word can be a token on its own (if the word is frequent) or broken into multiple tokens (if the word is rare). For example, in the first lines of Hamlet's monologue "To be or not to be," the SOTA GPT4 model treats most words and punctuation marks as one token each. However, GPT4's underlying byte pair encoding (BPE) tokenizer breaks rare word forms such as *nobler* into subword tokens, for example *nob* and *ler*, character sequences that often occur as parts of other rare words.[3]

There are several widely used subword tokenization algorithms, usually built upon the BPE method (Sennrich, Haddow & Birch, 2015). Models by Google often rely on the WordPiece algorithm (Song et al., 2021), inspired by BPE but built upon a proprietary technology. SentencePiece (Kudo & Richardson, 2018) can use BPEs but does not require word-separated input, applying to diverse languages and writing systems.

1.1.2 Transformer Architecture

Self-Attention   The *attention* mechanism originally gained wide acceptance in text processing in the field of machine translation as a useful addition to RNNs, starting from Bahdanau, Cho, and Bengio (2014). Later, Vaswani et al. (2017) introduced *self-attention* as the core mechanism for sequence processing that completely replaced RNNs. Self-attention allows for efficient training of ever-larger models on ever-larger data that was not technically possible with RNNs.

We reproduce the equation of self-attention here:

$$Attention(Q, K, V) = softmax\left(\frac{QK^T}{\sqrt{d_k}}\right) V, \tag{2}$$

where Q, K, and V are computed from the underlying sequence embedding M by multiplying it with matrices of numeric parameters: $Q = MW^Q, K = MW^K$, $V = MW^V$. The *softmax* function normalizes the scores that reflect the match between "query" vectors in Q and the "key" vectors in K, so that the weights for each position are positive and sum to 1; see the following example. Several self-attention components, called "attention heads," are computed in parallel

---

[3] For a visual demonstration, see https://platform.openai.com/tokenizer.

and combined into "multihead attention" *Multihead*, which is then combined with the input embedding matrix M via the residual connection, giving $M +$ *Multihead*(M) as output.

Informally, self-attention copies to a given token vector m_k information from token vectors at other positions. The tokens to be copied from are determined by the match between the query vector of token m_k from matrix Q, and the key vectors of all tokens from matrix K.

For example, take input M to encode text as a sequence of numeric vectors:

−7	−1	−10	−7
−1	−4	5	2
−6	6	2	7
the	cat	is	sitting

Vectors encoding tokens can be similar to each other across some or all dimensions. The vectors for *is* and *sitting* are the most similar. For example, the sign of all their vector components is the same: negative for the first dimension and positive for the others. Numbers in token vectors can encode semantic and syntactic information – for example, the second dimension could partly encode part of speech, with positive values for verbs.

A match between queries and keys is computed as QK^T, which after applying vector size and softmax normalization gives an *attention matrix* – for example:

0	0	0	0
0.99	0.01	0.86	0
0.01	0.19	0.14	1
0	0.8	0	0

The attention matrix specifies how much update each token's vector receives from different tokens. In our example, the last token *sitting* gets its entire update from token *is*, while token *the* receives 89 percent of the update from *cat*.

The values of the updates are taken from a separate matrix V – for example:

−8.7	2.4	2.3	5.8
−5.5	1.1	−2.6	0.01
−8	−3.6	−3	−2.5
the	cat	is	sitting

The attention update

2.3	5.1	2.3	2.3
1.1	−0.49	0.59	−2.6
−3.6	−2.6	−3.6	−3
the	cat	is	sitting

is added to the input.

After self-attention, the vector representations become more contextualized. In our toy example, both *the* and *is* received most of their attention update from *cat*. As a result, the vectors of *the* and *is* now signal aspects of their relation to the word *cat*. Being updated with similar information, these tokens also become more similar to each other:

$$
\begin{vmatrix}
-4.7 & 4.1 & -7.7 & -4.7 \\
0.1 & -4.5 & 5.6 & -0.6 \\
-9.7 & 3.4 & -1.6 & 4 \\
\text{the} & \text{cat} & \text{is} & \text{sitting}
\end{vmatrix}
$$

There are several other kinds of computation steps in Transformers, but self-attention is central. Informally, self-attention allows for information flow between positions in the sequence by selecting which positions to copy information from (via K to Q matching) and what form this information takes (via the V matrix). Roughly speaking, self-attention is the operation of selecting positions according to features in K and copying features from V. Components of self-attention specify the source, target, and nature of the copied information. For instance, Transformers could naturally approximate rules like "copy into the vector of a verb (encoded in Q) ontological semantic features (V) from the closest noun to the left (K)."

Other Transformer Components   In addition to the core self-attention mechanism that drives contextualization of word or token representations, there are several other components to the computation. Each of the components contributes nontrivially to the vector output values of the Transformer (Mickus, Paperno, & Constant, 2022).

For example, *layer normalization* is applied to intermediate vector representations at various points of computation. Every vector is scaled so that its dimensions have the average of 0 and the standard deviation of 1, making sure that no vector's dimensions take extreme values. This technique makes the training more efficient and reliable. It balances potentially unbounded contributions of other computation components, especially the feedforward step (see later in this section), which can introduce extreme vector value updates.

Positional encodings are another component required for the Transformer to work for natural language. The self-attention mechanism updates the inputs on the basis of their vector representations. If the input was encoded simply via word vectors, the Transformer would have been a bag-of-words model, ignoring the order in which the words appear. To inject order information, each token in the input is encoded as the sum of token vectors and *positional encodings*, special vectors uniquely characterizing the position of the token in the text. Positional encodings are designed so that nearby positions in the sequence receive similar positional encoding vectors. This allows self-attention operations to target not only word features but also positional features (e.g., "copy features from a preceding adjective to the noun").

Feedforward networks are interleaved in Transformers with self-attention and normalization operations. During the feedforward step, each token vector v (previously contextualized via self-attention) is passed through a neural network *FFN*, which consists of multiplying by two matrices of numeric weights and a nonlinear operation: $FFN(v) = W_2 max(0, W_1 v)$.

The result is added to the input via a residual connection: $v + FFN(v)$. The feedforward step is the one that introduces nonlinear transformations of the information about the current token and its context. Most of the numeric parameters of modern Transformer models correspond to the feedforward step. It has been argued that it is the feedforward networks that embody most of the knowledge encoded by Transformer models, including relational mappings such as correspondence between embeddings of present and past tense of verbs (Merullo, Eickhoff, & Pavlick, 2023).

1.1.3 Neural Model Training

Deep neural network models include a large number of numeric parameters that need to be estimated, or learned, from data. In the case of Transformer LMs, these trainable parameters include numeric values in vectors of all tokens in the vocabulary and in matrices that define the model's self-attention and feedforward operations.

Ultimately, large language models (LLMs) are evaluated on downstream tasks. For example, the natural language inference task often boils down to classifying sentence pairs as exemplifying an entailment, a contradiction, or neither.

Pretraining and Fine-Tuning   In modern deep learning models, a common approach taken in achieving state-of-the-art results in specific tasks combines *self-supervised pretraining* with task-specific *fine-tuning*, illustrated in Figure 1.

Typically, an LLM is *pretrained* on a distributional task, meaning that its output representations are optimized for predicting a match between the context and the textual element that can appear in it. For instance, the vector representation of a sentence can be trained to predict what continuations the sentence is likely to have. In GPT-like models (Radford et al., 2019), the training signal comes from predicting the next token in the context of the preceding sequence of tokens. In other models (like BERT; Devlin et al., 2019), token prediction happens in a bidirectional context (sentence with gaps), with tokens

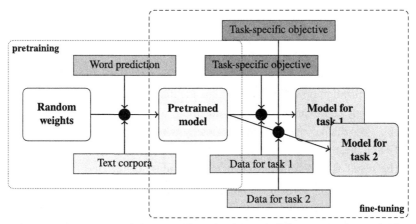

Figure 1 Two-step training paradigm: in the pretraining stage, the model is trained on large text corpora on a word prediction task. Task-specific training (fine-tuning) happens separately, with the pretrained model as a starting point.

to be predicted typically replaced by a dedicated [MASK] token. As such, the vector representation that is useful for token prediction cannot be immediately applied to alternative tasks involving reasoning, question answering, or sentiment analysis, inviting additional approaches including fine-tuning; see, however, Radford et al. (2019) and Brown et al. (2020) for influential views on the transfer of pretrained LMs to new tasks without such computationally expensive steps.

Vector outputs of a pretrained model can serve as input to a simpler neural component such as a feedforward neural network. The latter makes the actual task-specific predictions, such as whether one sentence in a pair entails the other. The whole pipeline can then be trained on the task-specific data (e.g., inference data), updating both the feedforward network's weights and the weights of the pretrained LM. The resulting *fine-tuned* LM differs from the original pretrained one, and produces task-specific vector representations of the input. Note that fine-tuning only produces reasonable empirical results when applied to a pretrained model, rather than learning the weights from scratch on task-specific data. One can think of the process of fine-tuning as highlighting the features of compositional representations produced by the pretrained model that are relevant for the specific task at hand, and suppressing irrelevant features. The intuition here is that the distributional pretraining allows the model to extract a wide set of features from the text, different subsets of which are useful for different downstream tasks. Features useful for one task (e.g., inference) may happen to be complementary to the features useful for another task (e.g., sentiment analysis), so instances of the same model fine-tuned on these tasks may prove quite distinct. Note that fine-tuning mainly affects representations at the top layers of deep models while the bulk of processing that happens in a majority of layers remains largely intact (Mickus et al., 2022).

Both pretraining and fine-tuning follow the *end-to-end* training approach: model parameters (weights) are not estimated for each module separately. Instead, even in the biggest models, all parameters are tuned in parallel, with an eye on how they affect the output in a given task. In pretraining, the output is the likelihood score assigned to the currently predicted token, and in fine-tuning, to the currently predicted other output such as the likelihood score of different classes in a classification task.

Fine-tuning a neural network on a dataset may lead to a loss of its generality. There is a risk that a model adapts to biases of the data on which it was fine-tuned, learning shallow statistical regularities. For example, the presence of the word *not* may be associated in a fine-tuning dataset with the example being a contradiction. A system fine-tuned on such a dataset may learn the shallow heuristic *not*⇒contradiction and fail to apply correctly to data from other sources where the heuristic is not helpful. For more discussion, see Section 2.

Methods for adjusting model parameters in neural networks rely on *gradient descent*. In simple terms, this means that each numeric parameter of the deep neural network is updated proportionally to the degree to which its change moves the model's prediction toward the desired output. Measures of discrepancy between the prediction and the desired outputs are known as *loss functions*.

Instruction-Tuning   Instruction-tuning is a specific type of refinement for pretrained LMs that has shown a distinctive potential since 2022.

An LM that predicts probabilities of tokens in context can be used for text generation. In this case, one may first estimate the probabilities of possible tokens, and pick a likely one to be generated. The newly generated token is appended to the context, and the next possible token is predicted. This text-generation process is called autoregressive decoding and exists in several alternative algorithms such as greedy decoding, nucleus sampling, topK sampling, and beam search.

Text generation is one of the tasks on which LMs can be fine-tuned. In particular, one can fine-tune LMs to generate responses to textual instruction. This is called instruction tuning. Furthermore, one can ask human annotators to rate or rank an LM's multiple possible responses to instructions. On the basis of human preferences, LMs can be further refined using techniques such as reinforcement learning (Ouyang et al., 2022). This approach underlies the creation of Chat-GPT and similar models (Touvron et al., 2023), which have proven effective at following many types of textual instructions.

Beyond Attention: Prompting for Few-Shot Learning   A possible bottleneck of highly parametrized compositional models is the amount of data required for successful learning. A modifier, such as adjective *red*, modeled as linear mapping from n-dimensional word vectors to n-dimensional phrase vectors (as in a lexical function model, see 3.2.2) would be represented via n^2 parameters (realistic case: $n = 300$, $n^2 = 90,000$). Learning compositional semantics therefore requires a wealth of data to estimate this huge number of parameters. In contrast, human learners need only a small number of examples to learn a new adjective and use it correctly with different nouns. Natural language compositionality can therefore be seen as a skill crucially involving *few-shot learning*. Indeed, few-shot learning behavior characterizes current LLMs (Brown et al., 2020; Patel et al., 2022). In case of the few-shot evaluation of LLMs, they are not fine-tuned on the task, but are provided a few examples of the fulfilled task as context.

```
necktie -> cravat
wave -> onde
```

Within that context, the model is tasked with continuing yet another example.

```
man -> _
```

The few-shot behavior of large pretrained LMs has been specifically demonstrated on presumably compositional tasks, such as question answering and unsupervised machine translation. The few-shot behavior of LLMs is not yet fully understood. Chan et al. (2022) argue that both the Transformer architecture and the structure of natural language corpora are necessary for LMs to develop the few-shot learning behavior. Olsson et al. (2022) argue for a causal mechanism they call "induction heads," a specific way in which an attention mechanism can explain the few-shot learning behavior.

Beyond Attention: Chain of Thought   Under the chain of thought, the model is prompted to produce the text of intermediate steps through which one can arrive at the output, which can help with recursion.

The following example taken from the Google AI blog illustrates the chain-of-thought prompting at work:[4]

```
Example input

Q: Roger has 5 tennis balls. He buys 2 more cans of
tennis balls. Each can has 3 tennis balls.
How many tennis balls does he have now?
```

---

[4] https://ai.googleblog.com/2022/04/pathways-language-model-palm-scaling-to.html.

Example output

```
Roger started with 5 balls. 2 cans of 3 tennis balls
each is 6 tennis balls. 5+6 = 11. The answer is 11.
```

In the example, only the last sentence of the output constitutes the answer to the question. The rest of the output only helps the model to arrive at the final answer. Indeed, chain-of-thought prompting improves the few-shot learning of Transformer models on tasks that involve multiple reasoning steps.

With this technical background in mind, we can turn to the second main ingredient of our survey: natural language semantics.

1.2 Theoretical Context: Natural Language Semantics

In this section, we set the theoretical foundation in semantics for the rest of the Element. Throughout the Element, we will talk a lot about "meaning," so we need to make this notion a bit more specific before we embark on the main discussion.

The nature of linguistic meanings and their place in the overall architecture of natural language grammar have been debated for millennia, and we will certainly not try to settle this debate here or follow its historic development (see Harris 1993 for an overview of recent history of semantics and linguistics in general).

Instead, let us take a different route: rather than directly asking fundamental questions about meaning, we shift our attention to more practical but related questions and let them guide us in building the theoretical basis for our discussion. Rather than asking "What is natural language semantics?" we can ask something like "How can semantic knowledge be detected in linguistic behavior?" On a more concrete level, instead of asking "What's the meaning of sentence X?" we can ask "How do we find out whether someone knows the meaning of sentence X?"

Take the sentence *A cat is sitting on a chair*. We know what this simple sentence means. This knowledge can manifest in a number of ways – for one, we are able to distinguish situations that can be truthfully described by this sentence from situations in which this sentence is false.

For example, given a schematic depiction of a situation in Figure 2 on the left, we can agree that the sentence *A cat is sitting on a chair* is true in this situation and false in the situation portrayed in the picture on the right – this is one of the ways our knowledge of the meaning of this sentence manifests itself.

As trivial as this observation may seem, it is the intuitive basis for the currently most widespread approach to linguistic meanings, *truth-conditional*

A cat is sitting on a chair.

Figure 2 Depictions of two situations: The sentence *A cat is sitting on a chair* is true in the left-hand situation, but not in the right-hand one.
Source: Images generated with AI image generation tool Midjourney, accessed April 15, 2023.

semantics. Knowledge of truth conditions of a sentence – the ability to distinguish situations where it is true from the ones where it is not – is under this approach fundamentally tied to the knowledge of what the sentence means. Heim and Kratzer (1998) open their classic textbook with the statement that equates truth conditions with sentence meaning: "To know the meaning of a sentence is to know its truth-conditions."

To sketch an implementation of this idea, let us think of sentence interpretation as a function I that takes two arguments – a sentence in natural language and a situation – and returns a *truth value*: *True* or *False* (along with whichever additional truth values your system is designed to have – for instance, the truth value *Undefined*). For our running example, this function will return *True* if its first argument is *A cat is sitting in a chair* and the second argument is the situation depicted in the left-hand side of Figure 2 (and it will, of course, return *False* for the other situation of the two, given the same sentence):

$$I(\textit{A cat is sitting on a chair})\left(\begin{array}{c}\text{}\end{array}\right) = \textbf{True}. \tag{3}$$

A different but related function I' would simply output the set of situations in which the sentence is true:

$$I'(\textit{A cat is sitting on a chair}) = \left\{ \begin{array}{c}\text{}\end{array}\right\}. \tag{4}$$

Both functions have their place in semantic practice. The latter can be used to pinpoint one possible notion of *the meaning of a sentence*: the set of situations where it is true.

Another core meaning-related intuition – besides the knowledge of *truth conditions* – is the ability to recognize whether sentences stand in a particular meaning relation to each other – that is, to draw inferences. Simply put, if we know the meaning of a sentence, we know what conclusions we can draw from it and what conclusions are not justified. Entailment – one type of *semantic inference* – is typically defined on pairs of sentences *A* and *B* along the following lines (Coppock & Champollion, 2022):

A ENTAILS B if and only if:

In any case where A is true, B is true too. $$\tag{5}$$

Note that both semantic notions corresponding to the basic meaning-related intuitions we discussed – *truth conditions* and *semantic inference* – operate on the level of sentences. Formal semantics as we know it has indeed been shaped primarily by *sentence-level phenomena*. This does not, of course, mean that no meanings are assigned to smaller linguistic units – phrases and individual words. But it would be fair to say that in this tradition, lexical meanings are viewed through the lens of their potential to combine into bigger units – ultimately, sentences.

Lexical meanings are therefore designed with combinatorial potential in mind: they need to be of the right *type* to combine into meanings of *sentential type* when used in a sentence. The sentential meanings, in turn, need to support evaluation for truth or falsity given a state of affairs, and to be of the right type for semantic inference.

We can now formulate the questions we will focus on in the forthcoming sections:

- How do deep learning models capture semantic relations between sentences? (Section 2 "Textual Inference")
- How do deep learning models build sentential meanings from meanings of smaller expressions? (Section 3 "Compositionality")
- How do deep learning models relate linguistic meanings to nonlinguistic information – in particular, visual information? (Section 4 "Grounding: Language and Vision")

Before we move on to the main sections discussing these questions, let us take a step back and have another look at the two main semantic notions that we have already introduced: truth conditions and semantic inference. Now, with some theoretical and technical background, we can elaborate a bit more on the role of these notions in semantic theory and in deep learning models trained on textual data.

Truth Conditions or Inference?   Which of the two notions – truth conditions or semantic inference – is taken as basic with respect to the other one defines the two views on natural language semantics that, in turn, provide two different perspectives on semantics in deep learning models. Let us zoom in on this a bit.

The currently most widely adopted version of compositional formal semantics builds on truth conditions – a view that can be traced back to the philosophical tradition that includes Alfred Tarski, Rudolf Carnap, Donald Davidson, David Lewis, and Richard Montague. As famously formulated by David Lewis (1970), "Semantics with no treatment of truth conditions is not semantics." Under this truth-conditional view – we will call it *referential* to contrast with its alternative – sentence-level semantics amounts to an association between sentences and sets of situations that make them true. Semantic inference relations within sentence pairs would then be mediated by sets of situations they describe: the relation holds by virtue of a set-theoretic relation between sentence meanings.

Objects that sentences are mapped to can have different specifics – they can be situations, worlds, circumstances, models, cases, etcetera, depending on the implementation. There is also variation among systems in whether the mapping between sentences and objects that express truth conditions is direct (Kratzer & Heim, 1998; Montague, 1970) or indirect via a representation language, typically some logic (Coppock & Champollion, 2022; Montague, 1973). The core of the referential view on semantics would remain the same: Meaning is defined by reference, understood as a mapping between linguistic objects on something external to language itself.

Alternatively, semantic inference relations (including but not limited to entailment) can be taken as basic – defined directly on sentence representations, without referencing the situations or worlds. We will call the view that builds on semantic relations the *inferential* view (Fitch, 1973; Lakoff, 1970; Moss, 2010, 2015; Murzi & Steinberger, 2017; Schroeder-Heister, 2018; Sommers, 1982; Van Benthem, 1986, 2008). This description groups together theories that have very important differences with each other, but, crucially for our discussion, they all capitalize on semantic relations between linguistic expressions (primarily sentences) as the core semantic notion.

The guiding observation for this view is that, given that people reason using language, the logical structures underlying human reasoning should correspond to the grammatical structure of natural language in a deep way. If these regularities are given central stage in analyzing meaning, reference and truth conditions can be explained as their by-product. This program can be summed up in two theses:

1. Meanings of linguistic expressions are determined by their role in inference.
2. To understand a linguistic expression is to know its role in inference.

The difference between the referential and inferential views is deep, but at the same time it carries mostly metasemantic value: it is a difference in the order of explanation and departing points such as formal and traditional logics. Radical versions of these views can also be seen as endpoints on the scale of importance of corresponding intuitions for semantics – those of truth conditions and those of inference. In practice, the views of most semanticists probably lie somewhere in between: grounding in nonlinguistic information has doubtless potential to enrich linguistic meanings; on the other hand, at least for some semantic phenomena, it is useful to directly examine semantic relations between expressions.

The importance of the referential/inferential distinction in the context of deep learning has to do with the fact that most of the deep learning models we will discuss are trained on exclusively textual data. This means that the representations these models develop are not referentially grounded to anything external to linguistic data itself (see, however, Section 4 on vision-and-language models).

The text-only training setup has stirred a debate around the semantic properties of LM representations. Do models trained on exclusively textual data develop representations that encode the full range of semantic information? Can tasks formulated as text-only be informative and useful for enhancing and/or probing models' semantic capabilities? We will now give an overview of this debate.

Grounding Argument against Semantics in Text-Only Models   Language is inherently grounded in a variety of extralinguistic experiences (Barsalou, 2008; Clark, 1996; Harnad, 1990; Meteyard et al., 2012; Parikh, 2001). Linguistic communication essentially involves a connection between what we say and what we mean, naturally implemented as a mapping between two separate spaces – the "what we say" and the "what we mean," respectively. The expression *the smell of coffee*, for example, describes a corresponding nonlinguistic olfactory experience. Can an agent that has not been exposed to the "what we mean" side of messages develop an understanding of what any message means?

The architecture of a lot of widely used computational models for language does not involve explicit mapping between text and "states of affairs" (although see Radford et al. 2021 and Section 4); they are usually not trained with the objective of mapping between object language and such model-theoretic space. This has led many to conclude that such models do not encode semantics at all – a conclusion that seems practically unavoidable under a referentialist truth-conditional view on semantics.

An influential position piece elaborating on this argument is Bender and Koller (2020), even though it might be a stretch to classify their position as strictly referentialist (their "what is meant" includes things like communicative intent, which is not really model-theoretic). In their own words, they "argue that the language modeling task, because it only uses form as training data, cannot in principle lead to learning of meaning." Since the language modeling task is that of string prediction, the "meanings" – whatever they are – are not in the training signal. Bender and Koller conclude that, for this reason, meanings cannot be learned as the result of this process, since LMs are not provided the means of solving the "symbol grounding problem" (Harnad, 1990) – that is, they have no means to connect text representations to the world these texts are used to communicate about.

To illustrate this position, Bender and Koller introduce a thought experiment that they call the octopus test, largely inspired by the Turing test for artificial intelligence (Turing, 2009). In the scenario, two people are stranded on two islands and are communicating via telegraph using an underwater cable. Meanwhile, an intelligent octopus underwater is eavesdropping on their conversations and, being extremely good at detecting statistical patterns, learns to predict the two people's replies to each other. Eventually, the octopus inserts itself into the conversation, successfully pretending to be one of the people. But when facing a situation that requires real-world knowledge of what a coconut is, the octopus fails since it knows nothing about the referent of the word.

Bender and Koller (2020) conclude that statistical patterns of co-occurrence cannot be enough to develop knowledge of meaning.[5] In the discussion that followed, other researchers cast doubt on this conclusion. Let us now review their arguments in favor of semantics without grounding (Merrill, Warstadt, & Linzen, 2020; Piantadosi & Hill; 2022; Potts, 2022).

Meaning without Grounding?   Consider a counterargument: It is one thing for a semantic theory to predict that text-based models should be unable to

---

[5] This argument applies to a different extent to pure LMs (trained exclusively for next-word prediction) and to models that underwent additional training on potentially more semantically grounding tasks, such as reinforcement learning with human feedback (Ouyang et al., 2022; Touvron et al., 2023) or natural language inference (Section 2). We thank a reviewer for this point.

encode semantic information – but it is up to the actual behavior of these models to either support this or suggest otherwise.

Following Potts (2020), let us shift our focus from a priori conclusions to a more practical reformulation: "Is it possible for language models to achieve truly robust and general capabilities to answer questions, reason with language, and translate between languages?" In this way, the extent to which the models can do so defines the extent to which they encode semantics (and therefore, have the capacity to achieve natural language understanding), regardless of the training data and objective.

There are at least two reasons for optimism. First, the general ability of deep learning models to acquire abstract information not explicitly given during training has been shown on, for example, hierarchical syntactic structure; see for instance the survey in Linzen and Baroni (2021). Second, empirically, we do not really know which types of input are necessary for humans to learn meanings and manipulate them. Visual grounding is clearly not necessary as congenitally blind people still acquire language (Landau & Gleitman, 1985); the same holds for smell (returning to the example with *the smell of coffee*), and so on. This does not mean that human semantic knowledge does not have a grounding component to it at all, but the extent to which human semantic representations can be constructed in the absence of different types of grounding suggests that the same can in principle hold of artificial learners.

Piantadosi and Hill (2022) address the same question from the perspective of conceptual role theory – a view on cognition in many ways close to the inferentialist semantic paradigm (see Margolis and Laurence 1999 for an overview of conceptual role theory and its alternatives). While acknowledging that the string-prediction training setup differs in format from human language acquisition, they review arguments suggesting that the meaning of a significant fraction of natural language expressions is primarily determined by the role they play in a larger mental theory rather than their reference.

Studies in language acquisition show some support for this idea: learning the meanings of various classes of words relies heavily on structural linguistic information (Gleitman 1990; Gleitman et al., 2005; Landau and Gleitman 1985). This is particularly true of expressions for concepts without observable correlates such as, for instance, verbs like *think* or *believe* (see Hacquard and Lidz 2022 for a review).

Taking this view to its extreme, a system relying on relations within one modality is not necessarily meaningless, with additional modalities providing various enrichments. Reference or grounding then adds to the "conceptual role" the word plays. The signal that the learner gets from text alone is already quite rich in conceptual role information, explicit and implicit. The task of the learner is to invert from observations to mechanisms that generate these data (see Merrill et al. 2022 for an estimation of how entailment could be learned by a text-only model under some simplifying assumptions).

This perspective, again, gives a practical turn to the question of semantics in text-only LMs: In order to know whether LMs learn to represent semantics during training and what it looks like, one has to examine the models' internal representations and how they relate to each other.

This practical angle motivates our Element: We will take a closer look at how these models perform on semantic tasks and examine the semantic properties of their internal representations.

The result can sometimes be disappointing: Despite the often-reported impressive performance of current deep learning models, upon closer investigation, it often turns out to be mere pattern memorization or bias propagation – and the sometimes "superhuman" scores on such tasks go down dramatically when the benchmark datasets are manipulated in a relevant way. At the same time, studies of LM representations reveal rich semantic structures such as color space geometry (Abdou et al., 2021) or the relative geographical positions of major cities (Gatti et al., 2022); some work shows indications that contextual representations of the latest text-only LMs implicitly encode models of entities and situations evolving as text progresses (Li, Nye, & Andreas 2021; but see Kim and Schuster 2023 for a critique of these results).

In this overview, we would like to give the reader a balanced picture of challenges and successes in this domain and suggest possible future directions.

We are now moving on to the main part of the Element. We went over both technical and theoretical background for the upcoming discussion. We introduced vector representations for words and larger linguistic sequences and discussed how such representations are usually obtained from deep neural network models, often ones based on the Transformer architecture (Devlin et al., 2019; Radford et al., 2019). We introduced the main notions and intuitions in theoretical semantics: truth conditions and semantic inference. Finally, we highlighted the tension between the text-only setup common in deep learning language modeling and the architecture of most common theoretical semantics frameworks that involve a separate interpretation space. This tension is the driving point for the rest of the discussion.

We will start the main part with an overview of reasoning and inference in deep learning models (Section 2), then we turn to compositionality (Section 3) and language grounding (Section 4).

2 Textual Inference

Studying semantic relations between sentences has long been the focus of linguistic semantics. When modeling sentence meaning, regardless of the choice between the referential and inferential views (see Section 1.2), one of the central goals is to license as many (correct) semantic relations between sentences as possible. For example, a semantic analysis of the sentences *A cat is sitting on a chair* and *A cat is on a chair* is inadequate if it does not license the entailment of the latter from the former.

The task of detecting these relations between sentences in textual form (*textual inference*) has been the most common way in NLP to directly evaluate to what degree an LM captures sentence meaning. This brings us to a popular NLP task that was originally referred to as *recognizing textual entailment* (RTE) and is currently known as *natural language inference* (NLI). Following Dagan et al., (2013):

> *Textual entailment* is defined as a directional relationship between pairs of text expressions, denoted by *T* (the entailing **Text**) and *H* (the entailed **Hypothesis**). We say that *T* entails *H* if humans reading *T* would typically infer that *H* is most likely true.

A Text–Hypothesis pair annotated with a ground truth inference label is called a *textual inference problem* or an RTE/NLI problem. The terms *Premise* and *Conclusion* are also commonly used instead of *Text* and *Hypothesis*, respectively. Originally, Dagan, Glickman, and Magnini (2006) proposed an NLP task on textual inference as a shared challenge called RTE.[6] They created a *textual inference dataset* – that is, a collection of textual inference problems, where they labeled the problems with *entailment* ($\Rightarrow$) and *non-entailment* ($\not\Rightarrow$) labels. (1)–(3) represent instances of the RTE problems.

(1)   About two weeks before the trial started, I was in Shapiro's office in Century City.
       $\Rightarrow$ Shapiro works in Century City.

(2)   Green cards are becoming more difficult to obtain.
       $\Rightarrow$ Green card is now difficult to receive.

(3)   The town is also home to the Dalai Lama and to more than 10,000 Tibetans living in exile.
       $\not\Rightarrow$ The Dalai Lama has been living in exile since 10,000.

---

[6]   A shared challenge or a shared task in NLP is a competition among NLP systems where systems are designed to tackle a common NLP problem. The shared task organizers usually provide training and test data for participant systems.

Although the RTE name and inference labels involve the term *entailment*, the notion of entailment found in the initial and subsequent inference datasets is a *softer* version of the logical entailment. This softness corresponds to the terms *humans reading*, *typically*, and *most likely* as highlighted in the definition just provided. For example, while (1) is considered textual entailment, strictly speaking, one can think of a possible scenario where a person has an office in Century City but does not work there. Another scenario that makes (1) non-entailment could be one in which Shapiro currently does not work in Century City but used to work there. However, during the creation of the RTE dataset, the authors deliberately gave little importance to tense in order to prevent a large number of problems from being labeled as non-entailment. In a similar spirit, (2) is an example of textual entailment, but *becoming more difficult* does not necessarily lead to being difficult.

Due to the mismatch between textual and logical entailments, Zaenen, Karttunen, and Crouch (2005) suggested using *textual inference* instead of *textual entailment*. Under the umbrella term *textual inference* they distinguish logical entailment from inferences triggered by conventional or conversational implicatures. We find their suggestion appealing and use *textual inference* instead of *RTE* and *NLI* throughout the Element.

Textual inference is an integral part of natural language understanding (NLU). Condoravdi et al., (2003) argue that detection of entailment and contradiction relations between texts is a minimal, necessary criterion for evaluating NLP systems on text understanding. A couple of inference evaluation datasets are a part of the standard NLU benchmarks GLUE (Wang, Singh, et al., 2019) and SuperGLUE (Wang, Pruksachatkun, et al., 2019).

Historically, textual inference was thought of as a potential module for downstream NLP applications such as question answering (QA), information retrieval (IR), information extraction (IE), (multi-)document summarization, etcetera. For example, in QA, a candidate answer should be entailed by a source text; in IR, a textual inference system can be used to validate a retrieved document based on its passage entailing the query phrase; in IE, the system should find a passage that entails entities in a target relation; a summary should be entailed by the source document(s). Despite these initial goals and expectations, the textual inference task became a stand-alone task over time. Due to the high performance of end-to-end models and the relative simplicity of their development, it is not common to use textual inference systems as a component of other systems.

In the next subsection, we will touch on several subtle and peculiar characteristics of the textual inference task as practiced in NLP. Then we will zoom in on a selection of semantic phenomena and corresponding datasets.

2.1 Things to Know about the Textual Inference Task

The inference capacity of LMs is evaluated on textual inference datasets. Let us discuss how such datasets are constructed and what kind of inference problems can be found in them. We will highlight several nonobvious properties of textual inference datasets.

2.1.1 Collecting Text–Hypothesis Pairs

Many textual inference datasets are created in two major steps: first, collecting Text–Hypothesis pairs, and second, annotating them with inference labels. The methods of collecting Text–Hypothesis pairs can roughly be divided into human-elicited, semiautomated, and fully automated methods.

The *human-elicited* method involves human annotators in creating an inference problem – for example, creating an entirely new problem, pairing existing sentences, or providing a Hypothesis given a Text or vice versa. Initially, inference problems in the series of RTE challenges were human-elicited by expert annotators and the organizers of the challenges. Due to the involvement of experts, the collection process was expensive and each iteration of the challenge prepared only 1,000 to 1,600 new inference problems. A step forward in the human-elicited collection came from Bowman et al. (2015), who created the Stanford NLI (SNLI) dataset, a collection of circa 570,000 sentence pairs. Hypotheses were written by crowd workers given a premise sentence and a target inference label. The size of SNLI has triggered a surge of deep learning models for textual inference. A collection protocol similar to SNLI was used to create another large inference dataset, multi-genre NLI (MNLI et al., 2018).

Semiautomated collection methods partially automatize the generation of sentences or automatically transform existing sentences. Manual work usually involves verification of Text–Hypothesis pairs on fluency or carrying out certain tasks that are difficult to reliably automatize. Marelli et al. (2014) were the first to semi automatically collect about 10,000 sentence pairs for the Sentences Involving Compositional Knowledge (SICK) dataset.

There are three main groups of approaches when collecting inference pairs with a *fully automated* method. The first approach takes advantage of already existing textual inference datasets and automatically *modifies* the problems. For example, Naik et al. (2018) modify MNLI data to create a stress test on spelling errors and various distractions (e.g., a high word overlap and length mismatch between a premise and a hypothesis). The second approach, as demonstrated by White et al. (2017), *recasts* datasets for other NLP tasks as inference datasets. The third approach automatically *generates* Text–Hypothesis pairs. This is usually done with the help of manually predesigned templates or formal grammar such as regular or context-free grammar. To automatically generate inference problems, Geiger et al. (2018) use the regular grammar in (4) to construct sentences. Optional elements are marked with ?, Q∈{*every, not every, some, no*}, and other grammatical category variables range over predefined sets of words.

(4)   Q   Adj? N   (does not)? Adv? V   Q   Adj? N

All these methods are actively used when collecting Text–Hypothesis pairs for new textual inference datasets. When pairs are human-written, one needs to be aware of potential biases that human annotators might introduce (see Section 2.1.4 for more details). Inference datasets generated fully automatically usually focus on a particular set of semantic phenomena and tend to have sentences with less structural or lexical diversity. Finally, semiautomated methods try to combine the best of both worlds to produce Text–Hypothesis pairs with diversity and at scale.

2.1.2 Annotating Inferences

Annotation of textual inferences means labeling Text–Hypothesis pairs with a ground truth inference label. Methods of annotating inferences can be roughly divided into three categories.

For *human annotation*, usually, crowd workers rather than experts or trained annotators are employed to produce judgments. The gold label of an inference problem is commonly set to the label that receives a majority of votes from annotators. For example, a Text–Hypothesis pair in the SICK dataset is labeled as entailment if at least three out of five crowdsourced judgments are in agreement. When annotating a pair, sometimes one of the inference judgments comes from the author of the pair. For instance, this is the case for SNLI, MNLI, and the datasets of RTE challenges.

Automatic annotation of inferences is typically used when inference pairs are fully automatically generated (see Section 2.1.1). When modifying or recasting an existing dataset, an automatic annotation method can simply map original labels to inference labels. For example, if an original inference problem is entailment, a new problem that is obtained by adding an informative and consistent conjunct to a Hypothesis will have a neutral inference label.

The third approach is to use *human annotations for a task simpler than inference*. For example, the Monotonicity Entailment Dataset (MED, Yanaka et al. 2019a) asks crowd workers to make certain phrases in a sentence more specific – for example, make *spectator* in *every spectator bought a ticket* more specific with *female spectator*. With the help of the human-elicited phrasal inference and the monotonicity calculus (see Section 2.2.2), one can automatically detect that the original sentence entails the new sentence obtained with the phrase replacement.

It is important to keep in mind that *not all gold labels are gold* (see Section 2.1.5). Human annotation might introduce erroneous gold labels due to insufficient annotation guidelines or ambiguity. For example, a substantial number of gold labels in the SICK dataset are inconsistently applied to the inference problems (Kalouli et al., 2023; Kalouli Real, & de Paiva, 2017; Marelli et al., 2014). The reason behind this is that annotators interpreted indefinite noun phrases in different ways: *A boy is running* and *A boy is not running* can be judged as contradiction or neutral depending on coreference or lack thereof (see Section 2.1.3 for more discussion).

2.1.3 Two Interpretations of Contradiction

The contradiction label was introduced at the third RTE challenge (Giampiccolo et al., 2007) as part of a pilot three-way classification of textual inference. Unlike the two-way classification in previous RTE datasets, the three-way classification distinguishes contradiction ($\perp\!\!\!\perp$) and neutral ($\#\#$) in non-entailment inferences ($\not\Rightarrow$). The contradiction label was defined in a similar vague fashion as the entailment label. In particular, according to de Marneffe, Rafferty, and Manning (2008), contradiction occurs when a Text and a Hypothesis are *extremely unlikely to be true simultaneously*. For the contradiction label, the annotation guidelines instructed that compatible referring expressions had the *same reference* in the absence of clear countervailing evidence.[7] This definition of contradiction worked well for the RTE challenge datasets mainly because the datasets kept Text–Hypothesis pairs grounded in natural data, which means that the pairs contained longer Texts and more definite NPs and named entities.

Annotation of the SICK dataset showed that if the co-reference of compatible referring expressions is not explicitly instructed for caption-like sentence pairs, crowd workers provide *mixed annotations* for the inference problems involving indefinite NPs and negation. For example, the SICK inference problems in (5) and (6) have the exact same structure from an inference perspective, but (5) gets the neutral gold label while (6) gets contradiction:

(5) A couple is not looking at a map. $\#\#$ A couple is looking at a map.

(6) A soccer ball is not rolling into a goal net.
     $\perp\!\!\!\perp$ A soccer ball is rolling into a goal net.

---

[7] https://nlp.stanford.edu/RTE3-pilot/contradictions.pdf.

Many Text–Hypothesis pairs are not in a contradiction relation if no co-reference of entities or events is assumed. Recall the example where *A boy is running* and *A boy is not running* do not form a contradiction pair unless *a boy* in both sentences refers to the same entity. If event co-reference is adopted, a pair like *A cat is sleeping* and *A dog is sleeping* would become a contradiction: The only participant of the sleeping event cannot be both a cat and a dog. Even worse, event co-reference would make *A cat is sleeping* and *A dog is running* a contradiction due to the incompatibility of sleeping and running events. Such a notion of contradiction is highly odd from a purely logical perspective.

To instruct crowd workers about annotating coreference-enforced contradiction, the authors of SNLI grounded sentences in photos without showing actual photos to the crowd workers. In particular, the crowd workers were asked whether a Hypothesis could definitely be a true, might be a true, or definitely be a false description of a photo whose caption was the Text.[8] Such a guideline prevents the co-reference issue the SICK dataset suffers from, but on the other hand, it introduces somewhat odd contradiction problems that involve unrelated sentences as illustrated by an SNLI problem in (7). It is important to note that problems like (7) are labeled as neutral in SICK. Hence models should not be trained on SICK and evaluated on SNLI/MNLI or vice versa as these datasets use different interpretations of contradiction.[9]

(7)   Dog carry[*sic*] leash in mouth runs through marsh.
        $\perp\!\!\!\perp$ A ship hitting an iceberg.

The majority of the existing inference datasets adopt the co-reference-enforced notion of contradiction. Several inference datasets are annotated with binary labels, entailment and non-entailment, and avoid opting for one of the contradiction notions.

2.1.4 Biases in Textual Inference

The main idea behind collecting textual inference datasets is to teach an NLP system regularities governing NLI or to evaluate its semantic capacity. However, high system performance on a particular inference dataset does not necessarily mean that the system has learned the underlying inference regularities. It might easily be the case that the system learned *accidentally introduced regularities behind the gold labels* in the dataset. For example, a high word

---

[8] Similar instructions were shown to crowd-worker annotators of MNLI, but the word *photo* was replaced with *situation or event* as, unlike SNLI, MNLI contains sentences in various text genres.

[9] Despite this, there are several works (we refrain from explicitly mentioning them) that overlook this mismatch between the interpretations of contradiction and jointly use these datasets for training and evaluation.

overlap between a Text and a Hypothesis is often a good indicator of the entailment relation, but it has little to do with the underlying rationale of inferences. Learning such accidental regularities might be easily overlooked in deep learning as models employ representations and transformations that are opaque for humans. Next we present two biases in textual inference datasets that further encourage models to learn accidental regularities about inferences.

The *hypothesis-only bias* is a dataset bias that allows models to achieve relatively high accuracy on the dataset while the models take only a Hypothesis as an input, completely ignoring the Text part. The hypothesis-only bias for the SNLI and MNLI datasets was concurrently reported by several works (Gururangan et al., 2018; Poliak et al., 2018; Tsuchiya, 2018). They showed that some neural models can correctly classify 63–69 percent of SNLI problems by looking only at a Hypothesis. This accuracy is twice as high as the majority baseline (34 percent).[10] For MNLI, the hypothesis-only performance range is 52–53 percent compared to 35 percent of the majority baseline. The root of the hypothesis-only bias lies in the data collection method of SNLI and MNLI. For example, in the test part of SNLI, 90 percent of inference problems with a word form of *sleep* in a Hypothesis is labeled as contradiction. This reflects the tactics crowd workers used to quickly provide a Hypothesis sentence per inference label. Using several neural models as examples, Gururangan et al. (2018) showed that after training on the datasets, the hypothesis-only bias gets projected into the predictions of the models.

Another common bias associated with inference datasets and learned by models is a *high word overlap* between a Text and a Hypothesis for entailment problems. The Heuristic Analysis for NLI Systems (HANS) dataset by McCoy, Pavlick, and Linzen (2019) intends to evaluate a model on the extent it uses a word-overlap heuristic for entailment classification. The dataset covers three types of heuristics depending on whether a Hypothesis is a subset, subsequence, or constituent of a Text. The entailment and non-entailment inference problems for each heuristic are given in (8). Note that every word in the shared Hypothesis sentence occurs in the Text sentences.

(8) a. *Subset heuristic*
         (i)   The cat with a collar slept. $\Rightarrow$
         (ii) The cat saw that the dog slept. $\not\Rightarrow$
     b. *Subsequence heuristic*
         (i)   The dog and the cat slept. $\Rightarrow$ The cat slept.
         (ii) The dog near the cat slept. $\not\Rightarrow$

---

[10] A majority baseline always predicts the most common label in a training dataset.

   c.   *Constituent heuristic*
      (i)   The dog saw the cat slept. $\Rightarrow$
      (ii)   If the cat slept, the dog was away. $\not\Rightarrow$

Several works (He, Wang, & Zhang, 2020; McCoy, Pavlick, & Linzen, 2019) showed that when neural models fine-tuned on large inference datasets are evaluated on HANS, the accuracy on (i)-style problems is much higher than on (ii). For instance, the accuracy gap is greater than 70 percent for BERT fine-tuned on MNLI. This indicates that the neural models have difficulties to distinguish high lexical overlap from entailment.

Besides the two mentioned biases, there are also other dataset biases. A *reversed word overlap bias* is a tendency to label a problem with a low word overlap as non-entailment (Rajaee, Yaghoobzadeh, & Pilehvar, 2022). Yet another bias is a *negation bias*, which is a preference to classify a problem as contradiction if it contains a negation word. The negation bias exists in SICK, SNLI, and MNLI (Gururangan et al., 2018; Lai & Hockenmaier, 2014). There is an entire research line in the textual inference that attempts to debias inference models.

2.1.5 Should the Textual Inference Task Be Categorical?

Textual inference is modeled as a two- or three-way classification task. But taking into account the soft nature of the entailment and contradiction notions, is a categorical classification suitable for textual inference? There have been at least two proposals for an alternative modeling of the textual inference task. One proposal models textual inference as a subjective probability of entailment while another one uses the distribution of human judgments over the inference labels instead of a single inference label.

Chen et al. (2020) argue for *uncertain NLI* (UNLI) where a Text–Hypothesis pair is estimated with a probability score rather than a single inference label. The probability score represents an average of subjective probabilities elicited from crowd workers.[11] An inference problem that gets the neutral gold label in SNLI but 0.84 entailment probability in UNLI is given in (9):

(9)   A man is singing into a microphone.
      (0.84) $\Rightarrow$ A man is performing on stage.

Nie, Zhou, and Bansal (2020) modeled the textual inference task as predicting a *probability distribution over the inference labels*. Following a proposal

---

[11] Note that the average might result in a probability close to 0.5 if annotators provide mixed estimates close to 0 and 1. To avoid such undesired results, one could opt for the mode or median of the estimates or simply drop the inference problems with such mixed judgments.

by Pavlick and Kwiatkowski (2019), they created the ChaosNLI dataset where gold standard distributions per inference problem were derived from 100 crowdsourced judgments. (10) illustrates an SNLI problem that originally had the entailment gold label obtained as a majority label from three entailment and two neutral judgments. However, after re-annotating the problem as a part of ChaosNLI, it gets contradiction as the most probable label in the label distribution.

(10)   The lady wearing a red coat is giving a speech.
        [(0.40) $\Rightarrow$, (0.01)##, (0.59)$\perp\!\!\!\perp$] Woman is the center of attention.

In total, 25 percent of the SNLI problems that were reused in ChaosNLI received a major inference label different from the original SNLI label. This indicates that the inference gold labels that are defined as a majority among several judgments are difficult to replicate and begs a question about the adequacy of the gold standard inference labels and the categorical nature of the textual inference task.

In the subsection, we covered several crucial characteristics of the textual inference task. We summarized common methods of creating datasets, namely collecting and annotating Text–Hypothesis pairs. During the dataset creation, one can control the interpretation of the contradiction label via annotation guidelines–whether to opt for the co-reference-enforced contradiction or a more logical notion that largely narrows down the contradiction inference problems. However, it is not easy to keep inference datasets free from biases, especially when the sentences are collected via crowdsourcing. Notable biases of inference datasets are the hypothesis-only bias and the high word overlap for entailment problems. Finally, there are inference problems for which a single inference label is not representative. While there have been at least two suggestions for abandoning a single inference label in textual inference, most of the inference datasets are still created as a two- or three-way classification task.

2.2 Phenomena-Specific Textual Inference

In this section, we describe several textual inference datasets that were created with clear linguistic and semantic phenomena in mind; in other words, they contain inference problems that require correct treatment of certain semantically heavy words or semantically peculiar constructions. Such inference datasets are usually inspired by studies in formal semantics. The list of the datasets is given in Table 2 at the end of the section. Additionally, we mention the results of

LMs on these datasets as reported by the original works.[12] Our focus on semantic phenomena-driven inference datasets distinguishes this section from other works that also summarize existing inference datasets (Chatzikyriakidis et al., 2017; Poliak, 2020; Storks, Gao, & Chai, 2019).

2.2.1 The FraCaS Test Suite

We start with the FraCaS test suite (Cooper et al., 1996) as it covers several semantic phenomena that have been intensively studied in semantics literature. The FraCaS test suite was originally created as a yes/no/unknown-QA test suite for NLP systems.[13] Only later it was converted and used as a textual inference test suite by MacCartney and Manning (2007). It contains only 334 well-formed inference problems but has nine focused sections covering generalized quantifiers (74), plurals (33), nominal anaphora (28), ellipsis (55), adjectives (22), comparatives (31), temporal reference (70), verbs (8), and attitudes (13). Background knowledge is explicitly encoded in the FraCaS inference problems as premises (e.g., *Every Swede is a Scandinavian*), and (multistep) logic-based reasoning is the only challenge built in the dataset.

The FraCaS inference dataset has been rarely used for evaluating LMs due to its small size and imbalance of inference labels (e.g., entailment covers 52 percent of the problems while contradiction covers only 9 percent).

As was already mentioned, the size and imbalance of the labels make FraCaS a nonrepresentative evaluation set. Its treatment of semantic phenomena and clear structure motivate new ways of creating inference problems and datasets. FraCaS is mainly used for testing logic-based approaches (Abzianidze, 2016; Bernardy & Chatzikyriakidis, 2021; Hu, Chen, & Moss, 2019).

2.2.2 Monotonicity

Reasoning with monotonicity is the most common phenomenon on which LMS have been evaluated. This is because monotonicity reasoning is well studied from a formal semantics point of view (Icard & Moss, 2014; Van Benthem, 1986) and captures inferences that can be characterized by phrase substitutions directly in surface forms, without translations into an intermediate formal meaning representation. This facilitates the automatic generation of inference problems on monotonicity reasoning.

Not all phrase substitutions in a sentence result in a new sentence that is entailed from the original one. With the help of monotonicity reasoning, we can identify certain entailment-preserving substitutions. This is done by modeling

---

[12] The results quickly get outdated given the fast progress in the field.

[13] https://nlp.stanford.edu/wcmac/downloads/fracas.xml.

the monotonicity properties of lexical units where quantifiers get the spotlight. Let us interpret the quantifier *most* as a binary function from unary predicates to $\{0, 1\}$ (for false and true, respectively), where it is non-monotone in its first argument position and upward monotone in its second argument position. This can be denoted as $most(x^\circ, y^\uparrow)$. Since *most* is upward monotone in y's position, inserting more general predicates in "most dogs y" should not decrease its truth value: "most dogs *are running*" $\leq$ "most dogs *are moving*", where $\leq$ can be interpreted as entailment. In the case of the non-monotone position of x, we cannot predict an order between the values of "most x are running" when two comparable arguments (e.g., *dog* and *pet*) are inserted in it: "most *dogs* are running" does not entail "most *pets* are running" and vice versa.

It gets more complicated when dealing with nested scopes of monotone operators. Let us analyze (11) as (11′), where each function is marked with monotonicity properties.[14] Following (11′), each word in (11) is colored based on its polarity – that is, the monotonicity property of the position that is a result of interference of monotone functions. Green (red) stands for an upward (downward, respectively) monotone position. When green (red) words are replaced with synonymous or more general (more specific) concepts, the resulting sentence is entailed from the initial one as demonstrated by (11)⇒(12); The results of replacement in (12) are underlined.

(11)   Every person without a mustache who consumed alcohol tasted most snacks.

(11′) $\text{Every}^{\downarrow\uparrow}\Big(\text{who}^{\uparrow\uparrow}(\text{without}^{\uparrow\downarrow}(\text{person, a mustache}), \text{consumed}^\uparrow(\text{alcohol})),$
        $\text{tasted}^\uparrow\ (\text{most}^\circ(\text{snacks}))\Big)$

(12)   Every <u>man</u> without <u>facial hair</u> who <u>drank</u> <u>whiskey</u> <u>tried</u> <u>some</u> snacks.

Textual inference datasets on monotonicity reasoning are usually (semi) automatically generated. The generation process goes as follows: (a) *Polarity marking* automatically detects the polarity of sub-phrases in a sentence by exploiting a syntactic structure and monotone operators in the sentence, (b) *Phrase substitution* substitutes polarity-marked sub-phrases with more general or specific phrases, and (c) *Entailment labeling* induces entailment relations based on the polarity of the substituted sub-phrases and the specificity order between substituted and substituting sub-phrases. Vanilla monotonicity reasoning cannot capture contradiction relations, hence most monotonicity-based inference datasets cover only entailment and non-entailment labels.

---

[14] Here, we adopt the quantifier scoping that follows the quantifier order in the surface form and yet yields a sensible semantic reading.

For the extension of monotonicity reasoning with an exclusion relation, see MacCartney and Manning (2009) and Icard (2012).

One of the first monotonicity-based inference datasets, the Monotonicity Entailment Dataset (MED), was semiautomatically created by Yanaka et al. (2019a). The final dataset contains more than 5,000 problems. While the problems are evenly balanced between entailment and non-entailment classes, underlying monotonicity phenomena are unevenly distributed: upward (34 percent), downward (61 percent), non (5 percent). The MED dataset is only intended for evaluation and comes with no training part.[15]

Yanaka et al. (2019a) evaluated top textual inference models at that time, including BERT, and found that the models underperform (below the majority baseline) on downward-monotone problems when trained on standard training sets, SNLI and MNLI. When augmenting a training set with the HELP dataset, the experiments showed that if a portion of the upward (downward) monotonicity problems increases in the training set, it hurts models to learn the downward (upward respectively) monotonicity reasoning. Chen (2021) reports the highest score by an LM on MED: a model with a tree structure encoder (Zhou, Liu, & Pan, 2016) and a self-attention (Lin et al., 2017) obtains an accuracy of 75.7 percent. A substantial improvement (93.4 percent) is reported by Chen, Gao, and Moss (2021) with a hybrid system that combines a monotonicity reasoning system with lexical databases and LLMs. However, such hybrid systems have an obvious advantage over purely neural models as they can faithfully mimic the algorithm underlying the creation of the evaluation data.

In contrast to the MED dataset, the monotonicity part of Semantic Fragments (hereafter referred to as monFrag) by Richardson et al. (2020) is fully automatically created: The sentence pairs are generated with a regular grammar using a restricted vocabulary of size 119 and following the polarity markings induced from monotone operators. Such controlled generation of the pairs backed up with polarity computation of Hu et al. (2019) guarantees correct assignments of three-way inference labels to the generated problems. monFrag contains 10K problems equally distributed over three labels and divided into simple and hard parts based on the number of relative clauses in sentences and the vocabulary size of quantifiers per part. A sample problem from the dataset is given in (13).

---

[15] MED was preceded by the fully automatically generated monotonicity inference dataset, called HELP (Yanaka et al., 2019b). Due to the automatic generation, which introduces some noise in inference labels and the naturalness of sentences, HELP is intended to be used as training data.

(13)   All black mammals saw exactly 5 stallions who danced ⊥⊥
        Some black rabbits did not see exactly 5 stallions who danced

As a result of their probing experiments, Richardson et al. (2020) found that LMs poorly generalize on monFrag, namely one of the best results is obtained by BERT: 62.8 accuracy score when trained on SNLI and MNLI. They also show that BERT predicts monFrag with 97.8 percent accuracy when fine-tuned on 2,000 similar monotonicity problems while its score decreases only by 1.3 percent on the MNLI development set.

Monotonicity reasoning represents a substantial challenge for LMs when it comes to distinguishing the reasoning processes driven by downward and upward monotone operators. While within the limited vocabulary (of ≈100 words) LMs overall learn the monotonicity reasoning in monFrag, generalizing monotonicity reasoning for a larger vocabulary remains a difficult problem.

For more details related to monotonicity and LMs, we refer readers to the following works: Yanaka et al. (2020) show LMs having difficulties to systematically generalize on monotonicity reasoning when syntactic structures in the training and test sets differ; Geiger, Richardson, and Potts (2020) demonstrate that BERT partially mirrors the causal dynamics of the algorithm that models a fragment of monotonicity reasoning restricted to negation and lexical entailment; and Geiger et al. (2018) emphasize the importance of alignment for reasoning with monotone quantifiers.

2.2.3 Negation

Understanding and processing negation is a challenging task for NLP systems, including those based on deep neural networks. The experiments by Kassner and Schütze (2020) and Ettinger (2020) showed that when using BERT as an LM to predict a word in a sentence and in its negated version, BERT shows little to no sensitivity to the presence of negation. Additionally, Ribeiro et al. (2020) demonstrated how inserting negation can mislead prominent commercial models for sentiment analysis.

Negation is present as a part of the challenge in most of the monotonicity reasoning-based inference datasets since it is one of the main sources of downward monotone operators. However, the complementing nature of negation is not fully captured by vanilla monotonicity reasoning. There are also synthetic challenge test sets (Richardson et al., 2020) and adversarial/stress sets (Naik et al., 2018) that focus on negation, but their coverage and the naturalness of sentences are rather low. Instead, we will discuss the textual inference dataset from Hossain et al. (2020), hereafter referred to as negNLI, which is a manually created and labeled dataset of size 4,500. It builds on the standard inference datasets such as RTE, SNLI, and MNLI.

The motivation behind creating negNLI was to test SOTA transformer models and their training datasets on the proper treatment of negations and their coverage, respectively. To create new inference problems, they extracted 500 Text–Hypothesis pairs per dataset (in total 1,500), added negation manually to the main verb of each sentence, and formed three new negation-involving problems: T_{neg}-H, T-H_{neg}, and T_{neg}-H_{neg}. Hence, negNLI consists of three subparts, negRTE, negSNLI, and negMNLI, corresponding to RTE, SNLI, and MNLI, respectively.

After experimenting with transformers such as BERT, RoBERTa (Liu et al., 2019) and XLNet (Yang et al., 2019), Hossain et al. (2020) found that the models underperform on negNLI when trained on the standard inference datasets. The results of these experiments are negative despite the problems in the subparts of negNLI being very similar to the original inference problems, differing only in terms of inserted negation particles.

Another inference dataset on negation worth mentioning is the NaN-NLI test suite (Truong et al., 2022), where NaN stands for Not another Negation. It is a small curated set of 258 inference problems and is intended only for evaluation use. The distinct feature of NaN-NLI is that it covers types of negation that rarely affect the inference labels in the datasets: nonverbal (e.g., *not all* and *not very*) and sub-clausal (e.g., negating a prepositional phrase as in *not for the first time*). The premises in the dataset are drawn from Pullum & Huddleston (2002). For each premise, the authors handcrafted around five hypotheses to form inference problems driven by a negation item.

In the evaluation experiments, Truong et al. (2022) use two pretrained LMs: RoBERTa and negRoBERTa, a variant of RoBERTa pretrained with negation data augmentation and a negation cue masking strategy (Truong et al., 2022). Both models are fine-tuned on MNLI and MNLI augmented with negMNLI of Hossain et al. (2020). The highest results are obtained when fine-tuning the models on the augmented data. The obtained scores of both models are comparable (ca. 62.7 percent) and represent a moderate improvement over the majority class baseline (45.3 percent).

Negative results on modeling negation are also reported by Hartmann et al. (2021) when evaluating the multilingual BERT model on five languages. Unlike previous datasets, Hartmann et al. (2021) structured their multilingual inference dataset in minimal pairs of inference problems. In this way, the dataset tests a model on whether it correctly recognizes the effect the presence and absence of negation have on inference labels.

Classifying textual inference problems with negation remains a challenge for LMs, stemming from the scope-taking nature of negation and its ability to flip the meaning of a phrase. The latter behavior contrasts with the general word insertion mechanism, which usually introduces additional information to the meaning (e.g., inserting adjuncts or complements).

2.2.4 Implicatures and Presuppositions

Implicatures and presuppositions are pragmatic inferences that are different from standard logical entailment. While implicatures are defeasible suggestions made by an utterance, presuppositions are assumed true by an utterance as they are essential for interpreting its meaning. Unlike entailments, presuppositions can survive even when they are embedded under questions, conditionals, and negation. For instance, (14) shows examples of a presupposition and an implicature (of the type usually called scalar implicature).

(14) Some of John's kids are playing outside.
      presupposes that   John has kids.
      implicates that   One of John's kids is not playing outside.

Note that the same presupposition would still be available if we considered the negated version of the sentence *Some of John's kids are not playing outside* or the question *Are some of John's kids playing outside?*.

The implicature in (14) arises because an alternative to *some* – namely *all* – could have been used, but it was not. Pragmatic reasoning about why this alternative was not used can lead to a conclusion from (14) that this alternative is not true (i.e., not all of John's kids are playing outside). The implicature can be canceled with the follow-up elaborating sentence *Actually all of John's kids are playing outside*.

The inference relation built into inference datasets has an imprecise definition that says "*T* entails (contradicts) *H* if humans reading *T* would typically infer that *H* is most likely true (false)" (see p. 21) and represents a weaker relation than logical entailment. This raises a question: What is the relation between the entailment that textual inference models learn and pragmatic inferences like implicatures and presuppositions? Do textual inference models recognize implicatures as entailment or as neutral? Are they robust enough to consistently accommodate presuppositions?

To answer these questions, Jeretic et al. (2020) automatically created an inference dataset, called IMPPRES, focusing on scalar implicatures and presuppositions. The problems were generated from predefined sentence templates, in total more than 25,000. The scalar implicature part consists of six subparts, each focusing on a particular lexical scale: *determiners* ⟨some,all⟩, *connectives* ⟨or,and⟩, *modals* ⟨can,have to⟩, *numerals* ⟨2,3⟩, *gradable adjectives* ⟨good,excellent⟩, and *gradable verbs* ⟨run,sprint⟩. The presupposition part has eight subparts involving *all N*, *both*, *change of state*, *cleft existence*, *cleft uniqueness*, *only*, *possessed definites*, and *questions*. As noted by the dataset authors, ImpPres is solely intended for evaluation purposes since the patterns in the dataset can be easily learned.

Experiments conducted on MNLI-trained BERT showed that with some consistency BERT uses pragmatic inference when *some* is in a premise – that is, identifies examples like ⟨*some N V, all N V*⟩ as contradiction. However, experiments on other subparts suggested that BERT cannot distinguish the scalar pairs for connectives and gradable concepts – for example, it treats *X is good* and *X is excellent* as semantically equivalent, and it inconsistently handles the cases of numerals and modals. Evaluation on the presupposition part reveals that BERT predicts entailment for presuppositions of clefts (e.g., *it is X who V* ⇒ *Someone V*), possessed definites, *only*, and questions (e.g., *John knew why Ann left* ⇒ *Ann left*) but fails to do so for numerals (e.g., *Both N V* ⇒ *Exactly two N V*) and change of state (e.g., *X was healed* ⇒ *X used to be ill*).

Jeretic et al. (2020) conclude that the pragmatic reasoning capacity of BERT mostly comes from the pretraining stage – that is, masked language modeling, as MNLI contains an insufficient number of pragmatic inferences and almost no samples of those triggered lexically. This leaves the question open whether LMs are able to consistently carry out pragmatic reasoning.

A follow-up study by Parrish et al. (2021) created a test dataset of more than 2,000 inference problems on presuppositions. In the dataset, the Text represents naturally occurring multiple sentences while the Hypothesis is manually constructed for each Text. To model the gradable nature of presupposition projection/cancellation, they also designed variants of Text that contain negated presupposition triggers. The results of their experiments show that models performed comparably to humans on relatively simple cases (e.g., cleft, numeric determiners, and temporal adverbs) but failed to fully capture human-level context sensitivity and gradience.

For related work, we refer the readers to Jiang and de Marneffe (2019), Ross and Pavlick (2019), and Schuster, Chen, and Degen (2020). Jiang and de Marneffe (2019) recast samples of CommitmentBank (de Marneffe, Simons, & Tonhauser, 2019) to inference problems, where the Text consists of multiple sentences, and the Hypothesis is a complement of clause-embedding verbs under entailment-canceling environments (conditional, negation, modal, and question). Based on the experiments with BERT models, they concluded that the models still do not capture the full complexity of pragmatic reasoning.

Ross and Pavlick (2019) studied whether BERT can make correct inferences about veridicality in verb–complement constructions. While the projectivity behavior of verb–complement verbs is different from presupposition projection, they share similarities when it comes to inferring embedded meaning. Schuster et al. (2020) explored whether an LSTM-based sentence encoder can be used to predict the strength of scalar inferences, namely predicting semantic similarity between *some kids play* and *some, but not all, kids play*.

2.2.5 Other Targeted Inference Datasets

In addition to the discussed inference datasets, there are many other datasets that focus on semantic phenomena beyond the scope of the section. Kober et al. (2019) designed and manually annotated a set of sentence pairs that require reasoning with *tense and aspect*.[16] Ravichander et al. (2019) prepared the EQUATE dataset for *quantitative reasoning* formatted as inference problems. Saha, Nie, and Bansal (2020) constructed the CONJNLI challenge set to evaluate LMs on understanding *connectives* (like *and, or, but, nor*) in conjunction with *quantifiers and negation*. In addition to the monotonicity fragment, Richardson et al. (2020) created synthetic data fragments for negation, Boolean connectives, quantifiers, and comparatives. Abzianidze et al. (2023) curated inference problems on *spatial reasoning* and showed that LMs are far from mastering it. Liu et al. (2023) designed an inference dataset, called AmbiEnt, to evaluate models on *reasoning with ambiguous sentences* involving a variety of lexical, syntactic, and pragmatic ambiguities. The dataset shifts from three-way classification to multi-label classification with three inference labels. Inference problems that are sensitive to the ambiguity of the Text are classified with more than one inference label.

2.3 Interim Conclusion

Since the first RTE task (Dagan et al., 2006), reasoning with natural language remains a popular NLP task. In the age of deep learning, the task gained momentum with the creation of the SNLI (Bowman et al., 2015) and MNLI (Williams et al., 2018) datasets.[17] Both MNLI and RTE (the merge of RTE1, RT2, RTE3, and RTE5) are part of the GLUE benchmark

---

[16] White et al. (2017), Poliak, Haldar, et al. (2018), and Vashishtha et al. (2020) together recast twenty datasets of other NLP tasks into inference dataset format. Their datasets cover phenomena such as temporal reasoning, event factuality, anaphora resolution, and semantic roles. However, the recast datasets have somewhat unnatural or uniformly structured Hypotheses.

[17] It also gradually got a new name, natural language inference (NLI), partially due to these dataset names and terminology used in the corresponding papers.

Table 2 A list of phenomena-specific textual inference datasets discussed in the current section. $t \times p$ in the size column stands for generating p number of inference problems from t number of templates. †A part of a dataset was used for training in the original experiments. "Dev" stands for a dataset having a designated development set. A list of abbreviations used: trained annotators (TA), crowd workers (CW), human-elicited (HE), and automatically/manually edited existing text (AE/ME). n^{σ} Multi-labeling with n number of labels.

Dataset	Size	Train part	Pair coll.	Lab. anno.	Lab. num.	Phenomena
FraCaS (Cooper et al., 1996)	334	No	HE	TA	3	Quantifiers, plurals, anaphora, ellipsis, adjectives, comparatives, temporal ref., verbs, attitude
MED (Yanaka et al., 2019a)	5,382	No	ME	CW	2	Monotonicity reasoning
Semantic fragments (Richardson et al., 2020)	40,000	Yes	Auto	Auto	3	Negation, Boolean connectives, quantifiers, counting, comparatives, monotonicity
negNLI (Hossain et al., 2020)	4,500	No†	ME	TA	3	Verb-level negation
Nan-NLI (T. H. Truong et al., 2022)	258	No	HE	TA	3	Diverse types of negation: verbal and nonverbal, clausal and sub-clausal, analytic and synthetic
IMPPRES (Jeretic et al., 2020)	25,500	No	Auto	Auto	3	Scalar implicature (six subparts) and presuppositions (eight subparts)
NOPE (Parrish et al., 2021)	2,732	No	HE	CW	3	Context-sensitivity of ten different types of presupposition triggers

Name	Size					Description
TEA (Kober, Bijl de Vroe, & Steedman, 2019)	11,138	No[†]	HE	TA	2	Tense and aspect: all combinations of present/past, simple/progressive/perfect and modal future, covering perfect, and progressive aspect
HANS (McCoy, Pavlick, & Linzen, 2019)	30×1,000	No[†]	Auto	Auto	2	Overlap heuristics: lexical, subsequence, sub-constituent
EQUATE (Ravichander et al., 2019)	9,606	No	AE Auto	TA CW Auto	2/3	Quantitative reasoning (five subsets): verbal reasoning with quantities, basic arithmetic computation, inferences with approximations, and range comparisons
ConjNLI (Saha, Nie, & Bansal, 2020)	1,623	Dev	AE	TA	3	(Non-)Boolean use of connectives (e.g., *and, or, but, nor*) with quantifiers and negation
SpaceNLI (Abzianidze, Zwarts, & Winter, 2023)	160×200	No[†]	Auto	Auto	3	Diverse types of spatial expressions: directional, argument orientation, projective, non-projective
AmbiEnt (A. Liu et al., 2023)	1,645	Dev	HE Auto	TA	3^{σ}	Ambiguity: sentences involving a variety of lexical, syntactic, and pragmatic ambiguities

(Wang, Singh, et al., 2019) for NLU. The new NLU benchmark SuperGLUE (Wang, Pruksachatkun, et al., 2019) dropped MNLI as by that time systems had already reached ≈90 percent of accuracy on the mismatched set, close to the human performance (92.8 percent). However, the RTE set was kept in SuperGLUE since system performance was nearly eight points lower than the human performance (93.6 percent). Currently, RTE's human threshold is already beaten by PaLM (Chowdhery et al., 2022).

Recently the NLP community started to actively create numerous inference datasets that focus on certain phenomena (Rogers & Rumshisky, 2020) to evaluate the competence of LLMs. This opened the door to two new evaluation modalities, in addition to the standard train-and-test regime: adversarial testing and challenge testing. While the former targets the weak points of a model to emphasize its brittleness, the latter tries to evaluate the model's competence on a particular linguistic phenomenon, which is usually out of the training set distribution.

Interestingly and somewhat unexpectedly, while the large models beat the SOTA on standard inference benchmark datasets (such as SNLI, MNLI, and RTE), new targeted inference datasets have been created that reveal the incompetence of these large models on a certain set of phenomena. Even if the models achieve human parity on (semantically) challenging inference datasets, there is substantial room for improving benchmarking in the textual inference task (Bowman & Dahl, 2021), which will significantly affect the evaluation results.

3 Compositionality

Compositionality of linguistic meaning is responsible for construction of propositional meanings from components put together combinatorially in tandem with the syntax of language.

Compositionality usually assumes a syntactic structure used as an input to interpretation. Typical deep learning models, however, operate on surface strings rather than syntactic structures. The assumption is that the relevant aspects of syntactic parsing are learned implicitly during end-to-end learning. This is plausible as neural models have shown good results in relevant tasks, namely recognizing recursive languages (Bernardy, 2018; Weiss, Goldberg, & Yahav, 2018) and learning constrained interpreted languages (Hudson & Manning, 2018; Lake & Baroni, 2018). Sometimes, instead of the general notion of compositionality, the more special property of systematicity is explored, for example, in Lake and Baroni (2018). Systematicity means extending semantic interpretation to combinations with new (atomic) lexical items.

Recursive compositional interpretation has been mainly explored on artificial languages of arithmetic expressions and sequence operations (Hupkes et al., 2020; Hupkes, Veldhoen, & Zuidema, 2018; Nangia & Bowman, 2018). In what follows, we review proposed methods of assessing compositional properties of neural systems (Andreas, 2019b; Ettinger et al., 2018; Mickus, Bernard, & Paperno, 2020; Soulos et al., 2020). Kim and Linzen (2020), for instance, include depth of recursion as one of the many aspects of systematic semantic generalization. We then explicate the computational processes and representations that mirror compositionality in SOTA computational models, most notably the Transformer.

The study of compositionality in current machine-learning models significantly overlaps with the study of *generalization* (Hupkes et al., 2022) as compositionality is the mechanism that enables semantic generalization to unseen combinations of linguistic elements.

Notions of Compositionality   Philosophers of language and formal semanticists assume a notion of compositionality for (linguistic) signs that goes back to the ideas of Gottlob Frege and his student Rudolf Carnap, whereby *the meaning of a complex expression is a function of the meanings of its parts and the way they are combined.* This notion, although argued to be rather weak (Kracht, 2011), imposes certain constraints on the nature of the underlying objects. Namely, one distinguishes the (linguistic) forms and their meanings and assumes certain combination operations applied to them. The assumptions of structure-building operations, while weakening the notion of compositionality, are nonetheless useful, because they allow for an elegant account for structural ambiguity; the sentence *Mary saw a man with binoculars* has two readings (Mary used the binoculars vs. the man had the binoculars), which are derived from combining the same words in different ways.

In contrast to this Fregean notion of compositionality, some researchers in machine learning and cognitive science discuss compositionality of concept representations within a model without necessarily a link to a natural or formal language that may express those concepts. Sometimes this is discussed under the name of combinatorial properties – for example, conjunctions of properties (the concept of being *round and striped*) are concidered compositional combinations of more basic concepts. Here, instead of (symbolic) linguistic expressions (such as the phrase *round and striped*), one focuses on learned meaning representations in cognitive or computational systems (e.g., the model's hidden states corresponding to round and striped objects). This literature (e.g., Tokmakov, Wang, & Hebert, 2019) investigates whether the system learned representations correspond to a *decomposition* of the inputs that are represented; inputs' combination is assumed to follow structure-building rules, explicitly building on the analogy with syntactic structure in language (Andreas, 2019b). For instance, Du, Li, and Mordatch (2020) compose properties of objects such as shape, color, and position for the purposes of image generation. Modern language and vision models such as CLIP (Radford et al., 2021) are known to learn the primitive concepts well, but concept compositions still fail to exhibit a correct treatment (Yun et al., 2022).

3.1 Tests of Compositionality

To a great extent, current neural approaches to language are black boxes. While architectures such as the Transformer are in principle Turing complete (Pérez, Barceló, & Marinkovic, 2021) and therefore capable of learning hierarchical syntax and compositional semantics accompanying it, they are not trying to implement these properties of language directly. Rather, compositionality is more of an emergent property.

Assume that a learner acquires a correspondence between language and a semantic representation. How can we tell if the resulting mapping is compositional? This question has been most persistently investigated in the study of emergent communication systems, – for example, Kirby et al. (2015).

A common method of measuring compositionality of the meaning-form mapping is correlation analysis, as proposed, for example, by Kirby, Cornish, and Smith (2008). It can be applied regardless of whether the meaning-form mapping arises via iterated artificial language learning in humans, or in computational simulations that may or may not include neural network models. The idea is as follows: If we have a similarity metric defined on linguistic forms (such as the Levenstein string edit distance) and a similarity metric defined on meaning representations (such as cosine of two vector representations of meaning), the similarities in form versus meaning should correlate. Pearson's product moment is used as a metric of compositionality. Alternative but related compositionality metrics have also been explored (Chaabouni et al., 2020). The correlation-based methods are of course a very rough measure of compositionality as defined in philosophy of language. If the meaning of a complex expression is a function of the meanings of its parts, containing largely the same parts does not guarantee relatedness of meaning. Indeed, functions can map related expressions to very different values. Take the example of predicate logic where each formula is interpreted as 0 or 1. An arbitrarily large formula ϕ can be very close to $\neg\phi$ in terms of the string edit distance (1 edit), but its semantic value is opposite.

But even when we stay away from extensionally interpreted predicate logic and close to natural language examples, meaning–form correlation appears to be problematic as a measure of compositionality. Common linguistic phenomena such as ambiguity and semantically irrelevant morphosyntactic variation can bring meaning–form correlation scores to very low values even in an otherwise perfectly compositional language, and meaning–form correlation as measured on naturalistic data is indeed strikingly low (Mickus et al., 2020).

3.1.1 Similarity-Based Tests

One approach to establishing whether compositional vector semantic representations are satisfactory relies on the notion of similarity. Vector spaces have inherent similarity structures that can be measured numerically with metrics like the cosine. The cosine values serve as the models' similarity or relatedness predictions for pairs of sentences or phrases, and are compared to numeric similarity or relatedness scores produced by human annotators for the same phrase or sentence pairs. Metrics of choice for composition model evaluations are typically correlation coefficients (Pearson's or Spearman's).

The first such similarity datasets were rather small – for example, human similarity judgments for adjective–noun, noun–noun, and verb–object combinations for 108 phrase pairs for each type in Mitchell and Lapata (2010); determiner–noun combinations (Bernardi et al., 2013) and sentences with transitive verbs (Kartsaklis, Sadrzadeh, & Pulman, 2013).

These small controlled datasets featuring dozens of phrases or sentences raise concerns of generality and ecological validity. They might not be representative of semantic composition in general. As a result, a model might work well for this data but fail to extend to other phrases or more complex data.

This motivated more ecologically valid datasets consisting of varied sentences with a range of syntactic structures. The Semantic Textual Similarity (STS) task, introduced by Agirre et al. (2012), presents sentence pairs annotated on a scale from 0 ("on different topics") to 5 ("completely equivalent"). The original sentences in the pairs were taken from a variety of sources, such as image and video descriptions and outputs of machine translation models. The SICK dataset (Marelli et al., 2014) tries to control for phenomena such as proper nouns that may affect model predictions but are distinct from composition and could confound the evaluation of compositional models.

There are also alternatives to human judgments on similarity or relatedness for evaluation of compositional representations. One proposal is that the similarity of vector representations of phrases should correspond to how often one of the components in the phrase is expressed by the same lexical item across languages (Ryzhova, Kyuseva, & Paperno, 2016). For example, the vector of the phrase *sharp knife* is expected to be more similar to that of *sharp saw* than *sharp needle* because across languages the former two consistently use the same translation for *sharp* (e.g., French *tranchant*), while the latter often differs (French *aigu*).

There is also the *rank approach* to intrinsic similarity-based evaluation. While ingenious, it has limited applicability and can only be used with vector models that can produce vector representations of phrases that are comparable to vectors of words. One can think of such a model as processing a corpus where every occurrence of the phrase *red car* is represented as a single token *red_car*. Such a model can then estimate a vector for the phrase *red car* (the *observed* phrase vector) just like it creates vectors for words *red* and *car* when they occur outside of the phrase. Ideally, an adequate composition model should predict a compositional vector for *red car* that closely resembles the observed vector of *red_car*. One metric of success for a compositional model is the rank: If the observed phrase vector is closer to the compositional one than vectors of other words and phrases, the model's prediction is on the right track and the rank is 1; if the compositional model is further off track, the rank of the "correct" phrase vector is higher.

Rank evaluation of vector composition was first applied by Baroni and Zamparelli (2010) and extended more broadly by Dima et al., (2019). See also Boleda, Baroni, McNally, et al. (2013) on adjective–noun vector composition for non-intersective adjectives.

3.1.2 Representation Testing on Downstream Tasks

Compositionality of models can also be estimated indirectly via downstream tasks. The assumption is that solving the specific task requires adequate semantic representations, which must be compositional. Such tasks include inference (section 2), sentiment analysis (determining how positively a text, typically customer feedback, describes a certain object), and QA (Rajpurkar et al., 2016):

(15)   **passage**:
        In meteorology, precipitation is any product of the condensation of atmospheric water vapor that falls under gravity. < ··· >
        question:
        What causes precipitation to fall?

Closely related to QA, the LAMBADA task (Paperno et al., 2016) is a fill-in-the-blank task where understanding of a whole passage above and beyond the immediate sentential context of the masked word is required to fulfill the task successfully. The LAMBADA task therefore approximately measures the ability of LMs to process compositional meaning of discourse. The LAMBADA task was challenging to all models at the time the dataset was introduced, but large LMs with few-shot learning on the task (Brown et al., 2020; Chowdhery et al., 2022) showed impressive progress on LAMBADA.

Such tasks have been instrumental in validating models; they all clearly involve compositional meaning. For example, a negation placed in a well-chosen position in the text can completely change the entailment relation between two sentences, the set of correct answers to a question about the text, or the text's sentiment. In other cases, a negation placed elsewhere might not interfere with the meaning of the text in the same ways, showing that proper treatment of negation requires compositionality: deriving the meaning of a complex text both from the elements in the text and the way they are combined.

3.1.3 Compositional Tasks

Toy Tasks   Researchers used dedicated toy tasks to study the ability of deep learning models to learn recursive compositional behavior. The Arithmetic Language task (Hupkes et al., 2018) consists in interpreting nested arithmetic expressions with + and − operations. For example, $((4 − 2) − 1)$ maps to the value 1.

Paperno (2022) proposes the Personal Relations task focusing on recursive composition in referring phrases. For example, learning systems are expected to map *Ann's friend's child* to *Donna* when trained on data that includes a mapping of *Ann's friend* to *Bill* and *Bill's child* to *Donna*.

Lake and Baroni (2018) propose the SCAN task consisting in mapping commands such as *jump twice* to action sequences such as I_JUMP I_JUMP. The dataset includes recursive structures like *jump twice and walk twice*. The SCAN dataset supports multiple data splits into training, development, and testing partitions. The most challenging one is the *jump* split whereby the training data contains the word *jump* only as the name of an atomic action I_JUMP while the test set includes complex examples with *jump* such as *jump twice and walk twice*. This split is intended to demonstrate true recursive generalization from simple to complex examples, as opposed to learning to fill gaps in large numbers of superficially similar examples.

Hupkes et al. (2020) developed a more complex "PCFG" task of processing commands that produce sequences, for example append swap F G H , repeat I J produces G H F I J I J: the sequence F G H gets the first element swapped into the last position and appended to sequence I J repeated twice.

In all of these toy tasks, deep learning models showed mixed results. On both the Arithmetic Language and Personal Relations tasks, recurrent models such as GRU showed good generalization behaviors, but only for left-branching structures, and robust composition with alternative architectures such as Transformers or CNNs has not been reported. For the SCAN task, generalization for the hard *jump* split has been achieved by custom modifications of learning models that have no (Nye et al., 2020) or only a weak independent justification (Chaabouni, Dessì, & Kharitonov, 2021). However, the chain-of-thought approach of Zhou et al. (2022) does appear to generalize to compositional tasks above and beyond SCAN. For the PCFG data, only some of the quantitative measures of compositionality showed high values for neural models.

Larger Tasks   Above and beyond intrinsic similarity-based evaluation and toy tasks, compositional properties of neural models have been explored in machine translation by Dankers, Bruni, and Hupkes (2022) and Hupkes et al. (2020), who argue that more training data makes neural models' generalization more compositional.

Kim and Linzen (2020) proposed the COGS dataset to test models semantic parsing: translation of natural language sentences into logical formulae that represent their meanings. For example, *A cat smiled* is translated into (16):

(16) $\text{cat}(x_1)$ AND $\text{smile.agent}(x_2, x_1)$

On COGS, neural models showed good generalization in cases that could be treated as lexical substitution but struggled to generalize to novel structural configurations, for example - created by deeper recursive syntactic embedding (e.g., *The cat liked that the dog liked that the mouse liked that the girl saw the rat*).

Srivastava et al. (2022) presented a benchmark of 204 language tasks (BIG-bench) that are supposed to go "beyond the imitation game" and test true linguistic generalization of LMs. Some of these tasks are designed to probe compositional semantics behavior, and they can include reasoning, as in the cause-and-effect task:

(17)   For each example, two events are given. Which event caused the other?
        choice: It started raining.
        choice: The driver turned the wipers on.

Many other aspects of compositionality in LMs are still waiting to be explored.

3.2 Methods for Compositionality

3.2.1 Levels of Composition

Compositional models exist for all levels of linguistic structure. For *morphology*, there were different attempts to use morpheme decomposition in computing vector representations of derived words (Botha & Blunsom, 2014; Lazaridou et al., 2013; Luong, Socher, & Manning, 2013). Vector-based representations are thereby learned for individual morphemes. Soricut and Och

(2015) combine a simple composition model with morphology induction. Most current NLP models do away with morphemes altogether. The simple and efficient fastText model (Bojanowski et al., 2017) approximates a word's vector as the sum of its character n-gram embeddings: rather than simply using the distribution of, for example, *hipster* across contexts, the system collects and sums the distributions of n-grams of characters – for example, *hips, ipst, pste, ster*. The contrasts in distributional informativeness of *hips* or *ster* versus *ipst* or *pste* might effectively approximate the effect of segmenting a word into morphemes. Another approach, standard in modern LMs, is subword tokenization, which may or may not correspond to morphemes. At the same time, there is evidence suggesting that morphologically informed segmentation might outperform sub-word segmentation (Hofmann, Pierrehumbert, & Schütze, 2021). Among sub-word-based alternatives (including BPE but also others, e.g., Jinman et al., 2020; Pinter, Guthrie, and Eisenstein 2017; fastText remains a robust method for producing rare word vectors (Prokhorov et al., 2019; Vulić et al., 2020).

In *phrase- and sentence-level* composition, many earlier models relied on parse tree representations as input, and therefore featured recursive composition following grammatical structure (Clark, Coecke, & Sadrzadeh, 2008; Irsoy & Cardie, 2014; Le & Zuidema, 2015; Paperno, Pham, & Baroni, 2014; Socher et al., 2012; Socher et al., 2013). However, state-of-the-art LMs are instead trained end to end on text data without explicit parsing.

The general principle of having the same composition model for all levels of language structure up to the level of *discourse* has evolved as computational models grew more sophisticated. It was already present in latent semantic analysis (Landauer & Dumais, 1997) in the simple form of vector addition. Modern LMs such as BERT and GPT employ a much more flexible mechanism of self-attention that has the same cross-level coverage from tokens up to monological or dialogical texts.

3.2.2 Theoretically Simple Models of Composition

The Additive Model of Composition   Assume that two items such as words that have vector representations are combined. What is the vector representation of their combination? The simplest approach to vector composition consists in adding up vectors of component words together. Repeated addition effectively treats text as a *bag of words*, meaning that word order and syntactic structure are ignored; texts with the same words in them are processed identically. Despite its simplicity, vector addition is surprisingly effective and robust in practice. For example, the sum of high-quality word vectors outperformed more sophisticated approaches to vector composition in the study of preposition ambiguity (Ritter et al., 2015). Vector addition has been used as a method for arriving at meaning representations of phrases, sentences, and even texts at least since Landauer and Dumais (1997). More recently, sentence representations as summed contextualized token vectors from Transformer-based models were suggested (Cer et al., 2018). Additive composition is efficient for a good reason. Ultimately, dimensions of word vectors are used to predict in which contexts the word is likely to be used; this is the objective of word embeddings and neural LMs. This means that values in word vectors translate into scores of statistical association between words and their contexts, which are usually related to the Pointwise Mutual Information (PMI) score (Levy & Goldberg, 2014):

$$PMI(w, c) = \log \frac{p(w, c)}{p(w)p(c)}, \tag{6}$$

where $p(w), p(c)$ are probabilities of the word and the context and $p(w, c)$ is the probability of their joint occurrence. Under the idealizing assumption that two words' associations with contexts do not interact non-trivially, it follows that the sum of two words' PMI values for a given context approximates these two words' combination's PMI for the same context. As a result, if vector dimensions of words correspond to PMIs as they do in models like GloVe and skip-gram, then the sum $\vec{car} + \vec{red}$ approximates the distributional profile of the phrase *red car* (Paperno & Baroni, 2016). If dimensions of $\vec{car}$ indicate that *car* raises the probability of context c by a orders of magnitude, and dimensions of $\vec{red}$ indicate that *red* raises the probability of context c by b orders of magnitude, then the phrase *red car* plausibly raises the probability of context c by $a + b$ orders of magnitude. This suggests additive vector composition as a strong baseline to the extent that words' PMI scores are linear functions of their vector dimensions. For models that do not include log transformation in the calculation of association scores, as in Mitchell and Lapata (2010), pointwise multiplication rather than addition is competitive.

Parametric Approaches to Vector Composition   The additive model has clear practical advantages. However, its conceptual issues are equally obvious. For instance, addition is effectively a bag-of-words model, agnostic of word order and syntactic structure. Addition predicts the exact same vectors for sentences *Cats chase mice* and *Mice chase cats*.

This observation motivates various parametric approaches to vector composition. This means that the vector of the phrase includes not just vector representations of the words involved, but also additional numeric parameters. Such parameters can be learned from distributional properties of phrases that can themselves be encoded in vectors. One simple parametric approach that proved efficient in different evaluations such as Mitchell and Lapata (2010) is weighted addition:

$$\vec{AB} = \alpha\vec{A} + \beta\vec{B} \tag{7}$$

where α and β are scalar factors. For example, the phrase vector $\vec{redcar}$ can be computed by combining vectors for words *red* and *car* with different weights (e.g., $0.6\vec{red} + 0.4\vec{car}$)

In Mitchell and Lapata's experiments, different weight combinations were estimated for different types of phrases. the first component (adjective) received a high weight in adjective–noun phrases while the second component (noun) had a higher weight in noun–noun compounds. One problem of the weighted addition is its monotonicity. If relations between vectors are expected to be useful in predicting entailment relations between words and phrases, the composition system should allow for different monotonic properties of elements in composition. For example, the determiner *some* maintains the entailment properties between nouns it combines with while *no* reverts them; however, in the case of (weighted) addition, relations between *some dog* versus *some animal* and *no dog* versus *no animal* would be characterized by the exact same linear offset. In contrast, richer models of composition allow for both monotonic and non-monotonic computation, and more powerful transformer-based LLMs discussed in what follows are known to exploit context monotonicity (Bylinina & Tikhonov, 2022; Jumelet et al., 2021).

These issues of additive models of composition are addressed by richer parametric models, which allow compositional combinations to proceed in more differentiated, even idiosyncratic ways. Directly inspired by type-driven semantic theory, the Lexical Function model (Baroni & Zamparelli, 2010) treats one element in the phrase as a function and the other as its argument. The functions in question are linear, so composition reduces to the multiplication of the argument vector by the function-specific matrix:

$$\vec{AB} = mat(A)\vec{B}, \tag{8}$$

An extension of the lexical function model to higher-order functions includes using multidimensional tensors in addition to matrices (Grefenstette et al., 2013). However, the increase in the number of parameters brought about with the introduction of tensors renders such compositional models increasingly impractical, motivating proposals such as the Practical Lexical Function model (Paperno et al., 2014).

In contrast to Lexical Function and versions thereof, other highly parametric approaches apply matrix weights to both elements of the composition and related highly parametric approaches (Dima et al., 2019; Guevara, 2011; Socher et al., 2012, 2013):

$$\vec{AB} = mat_1\vec{A} + mat_2\vec{B}. \tag{9}$$

where the matrices mat_1, mat_2 can be specific for the lexical items B, S combined, or be shared across lexical items. Some studies, such as Gamallo (2021), experimented with a different compositional approach based on syntactic dependencies rather than constituent structure.

The problem with all the parametric approaches to vector composition is in scaling up to diverse use cases on arbitrarily complex examples. End-to-end approaches such as LLMs work better for most tasks. They are not only more robust as they scale up rather easily to bigger input data, but they also do not depend on parsing quality or efficiency, all while sharing parameters of composition across different types of constructions.

3.2.3 Composition in State-of-the-Art Transformer Models

Attention-Based Composition   Modern computational models based on the Transformer architecture have at their heart the self-attention mechanism, combined with feedforward neural network sublayers. There are many different instances of both self-attention and feedforward layers in multilayer Transformers.

In practice, this means that Transformers are naturally adapted to execute the simple and relatively interpretable vector composition strategies discussed earlier in section 3.2.2. Both self-attention and feedforward steps include vector addition and input multiplication by a matrix. As such, Transformers can easily emulate (weighted) addition, (practical) lexical function, and other simple methods based on weighted sums and weight matrix multiplication.

Ability for step-by step-computation (chain of thought) is also useful not only for reasoning, but also for complex semantic composition. Zhou et al. (2022) propose *least-to-most*, a custom version of the chain-of-thought technique that allows GPT-3 to achieve good generalization on SCAN from just fourteen examples, as well as two other simple compositional tasks. Drozdov et al. (2022) show further that *least-to-most* also helps in more realistic compositional tasks such as COGS.

3.3 Interim Conclusion

The problem of compositionality in neural systems has been seriously addressed long before the present-day Transformer systems. Already Smolensky (1990) tried to design a principled neural treatment of compositionality using filler/role decomposition, with final representations derived from combinations of vector representations of elements combined ("fillers") and their roles in the structure. More recently, Smolensky and colleagues attempted to establish such filler-role structures in modern trained recurrent neural networks (McCoy et al., 2019) and to enhance Transformers with explicit filler-role representations (Schlag et al., 2019).

There is active ongoing research on compositional generalization using vector-based and neural network systems. This includes methods for helping achieve compositional goals (e.g., few-shot prompting and chain-of-thought reasoning), research on testing compositional generalization (e.g., development datasets like COGS), as well as interpretability of the composition process. Ideally, a successful system will make correct predictions on examples that require compositional understanding of language (here some systems already show promising behavior, e.g., for SCAN), while also using vector representations that make semantic composition interpretable; the latter is a more remote goal, although analyses like the one by Merullo et al. (2023) already go in this direction.

From different strands of this research emerges ample evidence that the nature and the order of presentation of training data have a significant effect on the compositional behavior of trained neural models (e.g., Paperno, 2022). Chan et al. (2022) show that statistical distributions of data in natural corpora enable essentially compositional few-shot behavior of LMs. Akyürek and Andreas (2022) and Andreas (2019a) propose and test methods of generating additional training data (*data augmentation*) that helps neural models arrive at compositional behavior. In their experiments, improvements are observed for various tasks that involve compositional behavior, including language modeling, SCAN, and COGS.

4 Grounding: Language and Vision

So far, we have mainly been discussing capabilities of deep learning models when it comes to meaning-related tasks that are defined on text – and, consequently, can be formulated for text-only models. Let us now take a step back and return to the theoretical debate we introduced in Section 1.2: Can text-based models develop representations that contain semantic information, given that such models lack an explicit separate, nonlinguistic, space to ground language in? We concluded, both on principled grounds and based on empirical results of text-only models' behavior, that aspects of linguistic semantics are inferrable from non-grounded text. Are models with non-grounded meaning representations qualitatively inferior and defective semantically when compared to models that are trained to connect linguistic representations to nonlinguistic objects and structures?

While for some researchers the answer is a definite yes (Bender & Koller, 2020) and for others it is less obvious (Merrill et al., 2022; Piantadosi & Hill 2022; Potts, 2020), there is little doubt that information from additional modalities at least has potential to enrich models' meaning representations. This section explores such grounding: We will focus on models and tasks that involve language in combination with additional, nonlinguistic information.

Linguistic data can be grounded in a variety of ways: the models can be connected to knowledge bases explicitly storing fragments of world knowledge (Du et al., 2022; Guu et al., 2020; Verga et al., 2020); texts can be associated with visual data (Li et al., 2019; Lu et al., 2019; Tan and Bansal 2019), or even some representation of smell (see an olfactory model in Kiela, Bulat, & Clark 2015).

Reviewing all existing types of grounding in deep learning models is hardly possible within this Element, so we focus on just one type of grounding here: visual grounding. Vision-and-language (V&L) models have shown the most impressive breakthroughs recently, with the high quality of images generated by the newest text-to-image models and fine-grained textual control of the details in the image – see recent models like DALLE-2 (Ramesh et al., 2022), Imagen (Saharia et al., 2022), Stable Diffusion (Rombach et al., 2021) and others. Figure 3 shows the output of three recent text-to-image models given the same textual prompt as an example. These generated images look impressive at the time we are writing this Element, but they are most likely far from SOTA when you are reading this. The rapid developments in the V&L field in

Figure 3 Images generated by DALLE-2[a] (left), Imagen[b] (middle) and Stable Diffusion[c] models (right) with the same text prompt: *A blue jay standing on a large basket of rainbow macarons.*

[a]Generated on the https://labs.openai.com website, accessed October 10, 2022.
[b]Example from Saharia et al. (2022).
[c]Generated on the Stable Diffusion demo page https://huggingface.co/spaces/stabilityai/stable-diffusion, accessed October 10, 2022.

combination with new and easier ways to personalize V&L models (Gal et al., 2022; Ruiz et al., 2022), as well as addition of the visual modality to latest Chat-GPT, are attracting a lot of attention of wider communities outside of NLP and computer vision to mapping between language and images, which is, in turn, likely to speed up the progress in this area and drive the progress of these models as tools in digital creativity pipelines and beyond.

In the context of our survey, V&L models are most interesting not as a creative tool, but as a window into the role of extralinguistic grounding in linguistic semantic representations. They give us two streams of information: In roughly truth-conditional terms, we can think of them as "what is said" and "what is meant," ignoring obvious caveats. As Bender and Koller (2020) note, to solve the symbol grounding problem, it is not enough to just have these two spaces: In a hypothetical V&L model they use as an example, a model has access to both texts and images, but the training objectives for textual data and for visual data are totally independent from each other. Such a model is not expected to make a connection between the two spaces – for example, it is not expected to be able to perform non-randomly on tasks that require establishing a contentful relation between image and text, such as producing an image caption. For grounding, a training objective needs to relate the two spaces somehow, and there are different potential ways to formulate such a relation.

This section will not give an exhaustive overview of V&L architectures, tasks, and results – it is a blooming field that is only partly relevant for the topic of this Element. Instead, this section will aim to sketch a general idea of how grounding language in visual modality can be approached, and of the main linguistic aspects of such alignment.

4.1 A Grounding Strategy

Ideas about the best ways to connect text to images vary a lot, as do actual implementations – from rather loose connections in terms of similarity (CLIP, Radford et al., 2021) to two-stream models with additional connections in terms of cross-modal attention (ViLBERT and ViLBERT 12-in-1, Lu et al., 2019; Lu et al., 2020) to architectures handling data from arbitrary sources and modalities as one single stream (VisualBERT, Li et al., 2019; Perceiver, Hawthorne et al., 2022).

Let us focus on one particular setup – that of CLIP (Radford et al., 2021): It is one of the simplest ones, but also the one that proved to provide a good basis for more complicated architectures as one of their components.

CLIP is pretrained with a contrastive learning objective. What this means is shown schematically in Figure 4: given a batch of image–text pairs, the model

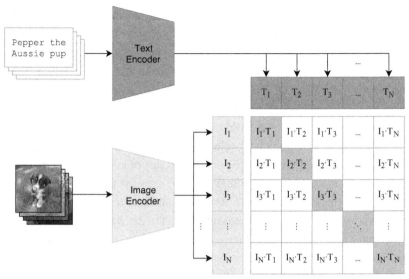

Figure 4 Summary of the core of CLIP training objective (Radford et al., 2021): contrasting matching text–image pairs with other text–image combinations from the same batch.

learns to distinguish the matching image–text pairs from the ones that do not match. Negative examples (the nonmatching images and texts) are constructed by mixing up images and texts from the original matching pairs. The model learns to distinguish matching pairs from nonmatching ones by jointly training two vector encoders – one for text and one for images – and encoding images and texts into a joint latent space where texts and images matching each other end up close to each other by cosine distance, and nonmatching ones are far from each other by the same distance measure. The learning objective for the model is to learn a contrast between such pairs, hence the objective name.

Part of the motivation behind this setup is the fact that there is a lot of data of this type – matching image–text pairs – available, which makes it possible in principle to leverage supervision implicitly present in these pairings to learn grounding of language in visual modality (CLIP is trained on 400 million image–text pairs). Note that the model that results from this type of grounding does not allow for text or image generation based on either modality – it is a bimodal encoder, which means that the only thing this model allows for without any additional components is to say, given an image and a text (or two images or two texts), how far they are from each other in the resulting shared space. This very simple objective gives rise to models that proved useful as parts of generative models – for example, CLIP text encoder is a component in the Stable Diffusion text-to-image model (Rombach et al., 2021).

An important question about the training objective is, of course, what are the properties of the grounding relation this procedure gives rise to – can similarity be reasonably seen as reference, or any other relevant truth-conditional notion? If not, what is the stronger training objective or model architecture that is appropriate for this role? There is little to no work directly addressing this theoretical question, but a relevant observation is made in Pezzelle (2023): CLIP-like contrastive pretraining gives rise to grounding that is sensitive not to truth-against-image specifically, but something quite different, a notion of "good description" of an image that is sensitive to the level of specificity of description that overrides truthful applicability. Real but wrong descriptions (coming from a different image) are systematically predicted by CLIP to be a better fit to an image than a description that is true but too general compared to descriptions typically found in training data – for instance, a nearly universally true description such as *They are doing something here.*

The space of possible V&L models and architectures is still waiting to be explored from the point of view of what kind of matches between text and image different types of training can give rise to (for a survey of Transformer V&L models, see Khan et al. 2021; on V&L models before 2019/2020, see Zhang et al., 2020).

But how do we evaluate the quality of the language-to-vision grounding? Let us find out.

4.2 Evaluation of Vision-and-Language Models

There is a vast literature centered around evaluation and interpretation of V&L models. These efforts and corresponding datasets can be organized along two axes: (1) the type of task used by the dataset; (2) which phenomena the dataset targets.

For a comprehensive taxonomy of V&L tasks, see Li et al. (2022). The most popular ones include textual output given an image or an image–text combination:

- **Visual question answering**: Given an image, the system needs to produce an answer to a textual question (Antol et al., 2015; Goyal et al., 2017; Hudson & Manning, 2019; Johnson et al., 2017; Suhr et al., 2017; Yi et al., 2019); for an overview of the linguistic side of visual QA, see Bernardi and Pezzelle (2021);
- **Image captioning**: The system generates a textual caption for an image (Hong et al., 2019; Mao et al., 2016; Vedantam et al., 2017).

Many of the tasks are applicable only to a subset of V&L models (e.g., those that have a decoder component – either image decoding or text decoding). Tasks that are applicable to V&L models across the board are those that solely rely on the output of text and image encoding – we can call them *matching* tasks. This type of task tests whether a model is able to distinguish between matching image–text pairs and the ones that do not match: for example, given a picture and two texts, tell which one is a better match for the picture, out of the two – or, conversely, given a text and two pictures, tell which one fits the textual description better. This type of task is defined, for instance, on a model like CLIP that was described earlier in this Element – a model that does not have a decoding component. Let us focus on matching for the rest of this section.

We will review three recent datasets organized in terms of matching for V&L models, centered around different linguistic phenomena, and how they are handled in models trained for visual grounding: VALSE (Parcalabescu et al., 2022), Winoground (Thrush et al., 2022), and ARO (Yuksekgonul et al., 2022).

VALSE (Vision And Language Structured Evaluation) (Parcalabescu et al., 2022) is a benchmark centered around linguistic phenomena that can be used to evaluate visio-linguistic grounding of V&L models. Each task of VALSE has the same structure: Given an image, a model needs to distinguish a real caption from a foil. A foil is a modification of a real caption, where a word or phrase is altered. The modification targets a particular linguistic phenomenon, and is meant to have consequences for visual modality as well as the text itself (i.e., has truth-conditional impact). VALSE covers the following phenomena: existence, plurality, counting, spatial relations, actions, and entity coreference. For existence, for example, the original caption might be 18a, and its foil will have *no* inserted, as in 18b. The picture associated with the caption–foil pair will have animals in it. The model should prefer 18a over 18b as a match for the picture.

(18)   a.   There are animals shown.   (Parcalabescu et al., 2022)
        b.   There are no animals shown.

Items for other target linguistic phenomena are structured in the same way.

VALSE data is sourced from existing V&L datasets with matching image–text pairs, with textual foils constructed using a combination of techniques, with additional filters that make sure that the foils are valid, are plausible, and do not exhibit distributional bias – in order to prevent models from solving the task disregarding the image, using just the clues from the text itself. As a final filtering step, the items go through human annotation. The resulting dataset consists of around 7,000 items in total, across linguistic phenomena.

Figure 5 An example from Winoground (Thrush et al., 2022). The images are expected to each match just one of two captions that contain the same words but in a different order: *some plants surrounding a lightbulb* (left) and *a lightbulb surrounding some plants* (right).

Out of five models benchmarked in the paper – CLIP (Radford et al., 2021), LXMERT (Tan & Bansal, 2019), ViLBERT (Lu et al., 2019), ViLBERT 12- in-1 (Lu et al., 2020), and VisualBERT (Li et al., 2019) – ViLBERT 12-in-1 shows the best results across the board. As for linguistic phenomena, V&L models are generally able to identify the presence or absence of objects, but struggle with everything else.

Winoground (Thrush et al., 2022) is a dataset with the structure of items similar to that of VALSE, allowing for model evaluation in terms of matching between images and text. Unlike in VALSE, the items consist of two images and two captions each. An item (images $I0$ and $I1$ and captions $C0$ and $C1$) satisfies the Winoground schema if and only if:

- $(C0, I0)$ and $(C1, I1)$ are a better match (and are preferred as such by annotators) than $(C1, I0)$ and $(C0, I1)$; and
- $C0$ and $C1$ have the same words and/or morphemes but the order differs.

The constraint on pairs of captions having exactly the same words is a consequence of the phenomenon the benchmark is targeting: The focus of Winoground is compositionality in V&L models – that is, how the meaning of the caption is built from the words used in it given the way these words combine with each other. Figure 5 shows an example of a Winoground item.

The dataset was handcrafted by expert annotators and contains 400 items.

Performance on Winoground is computed using three metrics: (1) text score (selecting the correct caption given an image); (2) image score (selecting the correct image given a caption); (3) combination of the two (every combination for a given example must be scored correctly in order for the example to be considered correct).

Evaluation of a variety of state-of-the-art V&L models on Winoground shows that all of the models rarely, if at all, outperform chance. This is an indication that, effectively, existing V&L models act based on bag-of-word-like representations.

ARO (Attribution, Relation, and Order) (Yuksekgonul et al., 2022) is a compositionality benchmark that contains about 50,000 test items and thus is more than ten times larger than Winoground. This allows for statistical exploration of the types of model failures on the subsets of data. ARO data is constructed based on existing datasets (Visual Genome, Krishna et al. 2017; GQA, Hudson and Manning 2019; COCO, Lin et al. 2014; Flickr30k, Young et al., 2014). The benchmark has four components:

- **Visual Genome Relation**: Relation participants are swapped in the caption (*the man is behind the tree* vs. *the tree is behind the man*).
- **Visual Genome Attribution**: Attributes in the caption are swapped (*the crouched man and the open door* vs. *the open man and the crouched door*).
- **COCO - Order** and **Flickr30k - Order**: Original captions are linearly perturbed in several different ways.

After testing an array of state-of-the-art V&L models on ARO, the authors confirm that the models fail at capturing any of the targeted phenomena, and basically act as bag-of-word models.

From further experiments, the authors conclude that the widespread contrastive training objective does not give the model the incentive to learn compositional information: For decent performance on typical V&L datasets, it is enough to learn some strategy that shortcuts past compositionality. They further propose a small fix for this problem: introducing hard negatives into training. Hard negatives are examples that are similar to actually matching text–image pairs but differ from them in a way that would only be possible to pin down if compositional information is taken into account. For captions, these involve NP or verb swaps; for images, this is achieved by including images very similar to the target image (according to some encoder, e.g., CLIP) into the batch during training. The goal of this is to enrich the notion of similarity between texts and images that the model develops so that it is more structurally aware. The reported results of such enrichment suggest that this is indeed a direction that can lead to higher compositionality.

Finally, good performance of a V&L model does not necessarily mean that the model has learned tightly coupled vision-language representations – it might not be relying on the two modalities symmetrically in its performance (see Frank, Bugliarello, & Elliott 2021; Hessel & Lee 2020; Parcalabescu & Frank 2022).

4.3 Linguistic Effects of Visual Grounding

General evaluation of V&L models, while providing insight about what models learn as a result of multimodal pretraining, does not answer the question of what the impact of an additional, visual modality on linguistic representations is. Despite the fact that V&L models are used in a plethora of downstream applications, there is still not a lot of work that directly compares their text representations to those of language-only models.

Studies making such comparisons almost unanimously report advantages of multimodal pretraining for the quality of text representations. Most evidence for the advantages of multimodality comes from similarity judgments. Text embeddings produced by V&L models give rise to similarity scores between pairs of words that correlate systematically better with human similarity judgments than scores from text-only models (De Deyne et al., 2021; Hill, Cho, & Korhonen 2016; see also Baroni 2016).

But there is also work that reports better performance of models equipped with language-to-vision grounding on a whole battery of classic text-only tasks. Tan and Bansal (2020) show that both BERT (Devlin et al., 2019) and RoBERTa (Liu et al., 2019), equipped with additional knowledge about visual counterparts of text tokens, outperform their text-only counterparts on all tasks included in the experiment – probably most notably, NLI tasks (QNLI and MNLI benchmarks; see Section 2).

Even though these results pointing in the direction of text representation improvement via visual grounding seem systematic and unanimous, it is often hard to reliably attribute the differences between models to the presence or absence of an additional modality – pretraining datasets for different models very rarely differ minimally (in presence vs. absence of images) – the textual component of data also differs quite a lot, captions being quite a special class of texts, linguistically. This makes targeted comparison between V&L and text-only models very hard. In particular, different types of texts might be subject to reporting bias to a different extent: Certain properties of objects (e.g., their color) could be under-mentioned in texts across the board, but also tend to be mentioned less or more in different text genres. Additionally, reporting bias is a potential source of weakness of linguistic representations in models trained only on text – but it is hard to disentangle the role of this bias in different aspects of pretraining. Zhang et al. (2022) focus specifically on reporting bias and whether visual grounding helps deal with it. They suggest a way to measure reporting bias by using information about co-occurrences in text corpora against visual co-occurrence extracted from Visual Genome (Krishna et al., 2017). They introduce the Visual Commonsense Tests (ViComTe) dataset with several property types for more than 5,000 objects. The dataset is exclusively textual and contains templates such as [subj] can be of color [obj], where one of the matching subject–object pairs would be (sky, blue). In a series of experiments, the authors test both V&L and text-only models on the task of matching entities with the correct physical attributes and conclude that visual grounding helps decrease the harms of reporting bias: Multimodal models perform better than text-only ones in reconstructing attribute distributions. Still they suffer from reporting bias, albeit to a smaller degree. Finally, varying model sizes did not have an effect on performance, which suggests that data is key.

Pezzelle, Takmaz, and Fernández (2021) look at V&L versus text-only model performance with particular attention to lexical semantics: Rather than testing text representations across the board, they partition their dataset into concrete versus abstract subsets and make separate comparisons for each of them. Like some of the previous work, they use semantic similarity as the window into representation quality, by comparing similarity measures derived from models to human similarity judgments. The results point in the direction of advantage of multimodal representations for concrete lexicon, but not for abstract words.

It is maybe not surprising that the impact of visual grounding is not the same across semantic lexical classes. The detailed landscape of these effects given different lexical semantic properties is still waiting to be explored (see, however, Tikhonov, Bylinina, & Paperno 2023 for some initial observations).

Among five models tested by Pezzelle et al. (2021), Vokenization (Tan & Bansal, 2020) exhibits the most robust results. This suggests, according to the authors, that it might be due to the way visual modality is incorporated into training. Unlike, for example, in CLIP (Radford et al., 2021), Vokenization aligns images with text on a token-by-token basis – each text token is paired with a corresponding image. Tentatively, this can lead to more fine-grained grounding, unlike sentence-level alignment seen in most other models, which might lead to less structured linguistic representations. Recall a similar complaint about text-level contrastive pretraining in Yuksekgonul et al. (2022), with hard negatives as a way to impose additional structure on linguistic representations.

Overall, different ways of evaluating V&L models seem to give somewhat contradictory results. On the one hand, visual grounding has been demonstrated to systematically improve linguistic representations. On the other hand, as shown by performance on V&L benchmarks that target particular linguistic phenomena that we discussed earlier in this Element, V&L models barely perform above chance. How should one make sense of this apparent contradiction? One possibility is that it boils down to the distinction between lexical and compositional aspects of linguistic representations targeted by different types of tests: Visual grounding helps lexical semantics, but it damages compositional properties of meanings of complex expressions.

To what extent this is a correct empirical characterization or an artifact of training data or objectives of particular models currently remains an open question (see, e.g., recent work suggesting that lexical representations in V&L models do not obey fundamental constraints on lexical meaning, in particular, ambiguous words can exhibit two readings at the same time, Rassin, Ravfogel, & Goldberg 2022).

Grounding and the landscape of its effects on linguistic meaning is an area rich in intriguing open research questions that can be given an empirical turn with the help of deep learning models.

4.4 Interim Conclusion and a Theoretical Note

We discussed deep learning models that connect linguistic and visual modality. We looked into one way of making such a connection and explored the resulting models. Before closing the discussion, a theoretical note is due.

Throughout this section, we treated images as something that a linguistic description can be true or false of. Practically, we looked at the space of possible images as a space of possible situations (worlds, states of affairs), which are related to sentences by the notion of truth. Recall the sketch of the interpretation function discussed in the introduction:

$$I(\textit{A cat is sitting on a chair})\left(\text{}\right) = \textbf{True}. \tag{10}$$

The function I relates sentences in natural language to states of affairs. This one particular state of affairs with a black cat sitting on a chair is shown by means of a picture in this equation, but that does not mean that the interpretation of the sentence *A cat is sitting on a chair* involves **the picture** – it is just a convenient shortcut because we cannot put an actual situation on a page as part of a formula. The picture simply represents it.

In fact, according to a prominent view, pictures themselves are content-bearing objects that can be input to an interpretation function quite like sentences in natural language. In *pictorial semantics*, pictures can be true or false with respect to a world and a bunch of additional parameters – quite like sentences in natural language semantics (Abusch, 2020; Greenberg, 2013, 2021; Schlenker, 2018):

(19)   **Truth of a picture**   (simplified from Schlenker 2018)
        A picture **P** is true in world w relative to viewpoint v along the system of projection S iff w projects to **P** from viewpoint v along S, or in other words: $\text{proj}_S(w, v) = $ **P**.

This setup does not support pictures as an interpretation space for language. Rather, pictures and language are two different types of content-bearing systems with (partially) shared mechanisms of semantic mapping on to an external interpretation space. This might seem like theoretical nitpicking, but taking the interpretational relation between different modalities seriously has the potential to guide architectures and analyses of models involving extralinguistic grounding. A connection between this theoretical view and practical work in shared V&L representations in deep learning models is waiting to be made.

5 Conclusions, Open Problems, and Further Directions

Our Element described the general landscape of semantics-related research in the field of deep learning. Deep learning allows us to develop computational models for what semanticists care about: (compositional) meaning representations, reasoning based on these representations, and language grounding in (visual) reality. State-of-the-art deep learning models are treating these tasks in quite crude ways, but are constantly improving and achieving good results on current evaluation benchmarks, which themselves become more and more sophisticated and hard to fool with simple shortcuts.[18]

Having in mind that our readers would typically have background either in NLP/computational linguistics or in theoretical semantics, our conclusions and thoughts prompted by our discussion could fall into two groups as well: (1) further directions of progress in semantic technologies; (2) relevance of deep learning models for research in theoretical semantics and for language theory in general.

5.1 The Future of Semantic Technologies

Training efficiency.   While modern deep learning models often show something like compositional behavior, they seem to achieve this in a nonhuman way. In particular, a lot of training data is required. Future progress in deep

---

[18] See code illustrations for the topics of this Element at https://github.com/kovvalsky/SemDL.

learning will permit achieving compositional solutions from smaller data. Few-shot learning in LLMs is already a step in that direction; however, the amounts of data and computation necessary for a quality model make this approach unsustainable.

Better evaluation. There is a need for a consensus on a principled set of evaluation criteria for fundamental semantic phenomena like compositionality or semantic inference. Linguists and philosophers of language can potentially have a significant impact here for the AI enterprise as a whole.

At the same time, expert-generated handcrafted datasets are usually relatively small in size and lack diversity. One natural direction in semantic evaluation is to use ensembles of datasets of different types.

Agent-oriented perspective. So far, the bulk of deep learning approaches in computational treatment of language focus on the modeling perspective. This can be in the context of *language modeling*, which creates a probabilistic model of the text, or language and vision modeling, which leans somewhat more in the direction of grounded semantics, with images serving as models for a textual description. However, the agency of the speaker largely remains out of focus. As a result, a wealth of meaning-related phenomena in language within the domains of deixis and pragmatics escapes researchers' attention. We expect this to limit the modeling of natural communication within AI systems. In the future, we expect further breakthroughs in the field to take into account a more complex communicative situation including the speaker's agency and intent. Linguists should take the lead in showing the way forward in these fields and designing datasets for development and testing relevant computational models.

From classification to structure prediction. While interpretation and semantic inference is a process, a lot of semantic NLP tasks are framed as classification. This only takes into account the final result and ignores the inner workings of the process. As a result, DNNs often learn shortcuts to predict correct inference classes instead of sound algorithms.

We can force deep learning systems to learn sound faithful reasoning behind the correct labels by making them learn the reasoning process that causes the gold label. This automatically yields systems that are inherently explainable.

Learning proofs and inference labels have been recently pursued by Clark, Tafjord, and Richardson (2021), Saha et al., (2020), and Tafjord, Dalvi, and Clark (2021). Unfortunately, there is no reliable automatic way to evaluate system-generated explanations of this type. We think that this is an important direction for future work.

Methods for comprehensive dataset creation. Due to the high demand for large data, all large (>10,000) semantics datasets are created with the help of crowdsourcing, data recasting, or automatic generation of synthetic data.

These methods are not practical for designing high-coverage datasets with comprehensive semantics-aware annotations. Collecting such datasets requires well-developed annotation guidelines and a group of trained annotators. This is practical in current settings as we already have examples of such large datasets with expert annotations: Universal Dependencies (Nivre et al., 2020), Parallel Meaning Bank (Abzianidze et al., 2017), and Abstract Meaning Representation corpora (Banarescu et al., 2013).

Recently Dalvi et al. (2021) collected about 1,800 multistep entailment trees that represent proof trees where children nodes collectively entail the parent node.[19] Putting more resources and leveraging crowdsourcing for developing such annotation-rich datasets targeting semantic phenomena will result in more comprehensive training and evaluation.

5.2 The Future of Semantic Research

Between language, neural models, and linguistic theory. There is a lot of work in the general field of deep net interpretability that probes the linguistic knowledge of LMs (see, e.g., Rogers, Kovaleva, and Rumshisky 2020 for an overview). These are experiments that establish the degree, quality, and limits of linguistic generalizations exhibited by, for example, models like BERT or GPT. Despite the growing amount of such work, its results have barely had any consequence for theories and analyses in theoretical linguistics, including theoretical semantics.

The reason, we believe, is mainly methodological: What is the place of the results of LM interpretability experiments in the process of constructing or revising linguistic theories? If a certain linguistic property of LM representations is discovered as a result of probing, why would language theory care? After all, this does not say anything about how people represent language, at least not directly.

There are several potential answers to this methodological stumbling block.

DNNs as theories. The first potential answer suggests treating models themselves as linguistic theories, albeit very different from the ones we are used to in theoretical linguistics at the moment (Baroni, 2022). Models' representations and weights that result from exposure to training data can be seen as ways of making sense of this data that also come with means to make predictions about new data (e.g., expectations about sentence acceptability). In this way, LMs can be seen as algorithmic linguistic theories. Manipulating different properties of models and training data in different ways and exploring the effects of such

---

[19] As they report, it took in total circa 600 hours of work carried out by three graduate and undergraduate annotators.

manipulations on the resulting "algorithmic theory" can uncover causal links between prominent generalizations and data or structures that trigger them.

Modeling of acquisition and learnability. This leads to learnability and language acquisition – another area where deep learning can be particularly helpful. Artificial learners such as deep nets can be used in testing which settings or which types of data or learning curricula lead to more humanlike language acquisition trajectories and results (Warstadt & Bowman, 2022). This, in turn, allows us to reverse-engineer hypotheses about mechanisms used by human language learners.

Finally, uncovering systematic misalignments between linguistic "knowledge" of neural LMs and implicit generalizations that guide humans' linguistic behavior is important for the learnability debate (Davis, 2022). Are there aspects of language, and, in particular, linguistic meanings, that can never be learned successfully by learning agents only exposed to texts, regardless of the model architecture or the amount of data? If yes, what do these aspects of language rely on? Would visual grounding be enough for successful learning? Maybe some meanings crucially rely on world knowledge or communicative reinforcement. These are all questions that are crucial for shaping our theories of meaning and language, and deep learning models provide rich experimental ground for theoretical advances in this domain.

References

Abdou, M., Kulmizev, A., Hershcovich, D., et al. (2021). Can language models encode perceptual structure without grounding? A case study in color. *arXiv:2109.06129.*

Abusch, D. (2020). Possible-worlds semantics for pictures. In D. Gutzmann, L. Matthewson, C. Meier, et al., eds., *The Wiley Blackwell companion to semantics* (pp. 1–31). Wiley Blackwell.

Abzianidze, L. (2016). Natural solution to fracas entailment problems. In *Proceedings of *SEM* (pp. 64–74). ACL.

Abzianidze, L., Bjerva, J., Evang, K., et al. (2017). The Parallel Meaning Bank: Towards a multilingual corpus of translations annotated with compositional meaning representations. In *Proceedings of EACL* (pp. 242–247). ACL.

Abzianidze, L., Zwarts, J., & Winter, Y. (2023). SpaceNLI: Evaluating the consistency of predicting inferences in space. In *Proceedings of NALOMA* (pp. 12–24). ACL.

Agirre, E., Cer, D., Diab, M., & Gonzalez-Agirre, A. (2012). Semeval-2012 task 6: A pilot on semantic textual similarity. In *Proceedings of Semeval* (pp. 385–393).

Akyürek, E., & Andreas, J. (2022). Compositionality as lexical symmetry. *arXiv:2201.12926.*

Andreas, J. (2019a). Good-enough compositional data augmentation. *arXiv: 1904.09545.*

Andreas, J. (2019b). Measuring compositionality in representation learning. In *International conference on learning representations.* https://openreview .net/forum?id=HJz05o0qK7.

Antol, S., Agrawal, A., Lu, J., et al. (2015). Vqa: Visual question answering. In *Proceedings of IEEE/CVFICCV* (pp. 2425–2433).

Bahdanau, D., Cho, K., & Bengio, Y. (2014). Neural machine translation by jointly learning to align and translate. *arXiv:1409.0473.*

Banarescu, L., Bonial, C., Cai, S., et al. (2013). Abstract meaning representation for sembanking. In *Proceedings of the 7th linguistic annotation workshop and interoperability with discourse* (pp. 178–186). ACL.

Baroni, M. (2016). Grounding distributional semantics in the visual world. *Language and Linguistics Compass, 10*(1), 3–13.

Baroni, M. (2022). On the proper role of linguistically-oriented deep net analysis in linguistic theorizing. In S. Lappin, ed., *Algebraic systems and the representation of linguistic knowledge* (pp. 5–22). Taylor and Francis.

Baroni, M., Dinu, G., & Kruszewski, G. (2014). Don't count, predict! A systematic comparison of context-counting vs. context-predicting semantic vectors. In *Proceedings of ACL* (pp. 238–247). ACL.

Baroni, M., & Zamparelli, R. (2010). Nouns are vectors, adjectives are matrices: Representing adjective–noun constructions in semantic space. In *Proceedings of EMNLP* (pp. 1183–1193).

Barsalou, L. W. (2008). Grounded cognition. *Annual Review of Psychology*, *59*(1), 617–645.

Bender, E. M., & Koller, A. (2020). Climbing towards NLU: On meaning, form, and understanding in the age of data. In *Proceedings of ACL* (pp. 5185–5198). ACL.

Bernardi, R., Dinu, G., Marelli, M., & Baroni, M. (2013). A relatedness benchmark to test the role of determiners in compositional distributional semantics. In *Proceedings of ACL* (pp. 53–57). ACL.

Bernardi, R., & Pezzelle, S. (2021). Linguistic issues behind visual question answering. *Language and Linguistics Compass*, *15*(6), e12417.

Bernardy, J.-P. (2018). Can recurrent neural networks learn nested recursion? *Linguistic Issues in Language Technology*, *16*(1). https://aclanthology.org/2018.lilt-16.1.

Bernardy, J.-P., & Chatzikyriakidis, S. (2021). Applied temporal analysis: A complete run of the FraCaS test suite. In *Proceedings of IWCS* (pp. 11–20). ACL.

Bojanowski, P., Grave, E., Joulin, A., & Mikolov, T. (2017). Enriching word vectors with subword information. *Transactions of the Association for Computational Linguistics*, *5*, 135–146.

Boleda, G., Baroni, M., McNally, L., et al. (2013). Intensionality was only alleged: On adjective-noun composition in distributional semantics. In *Proceedings of IWCS*.

Botha, J., & Blunsom, P. (2014). Compositional morphology for word representations and language modelling. In E. P. Xing & T. Jebara, eds., *Proceedings of the 31st international conference on machine learning* (Vol. 32, no. 2) (pp. 1899–1907). https://proceedings.mlr.press/v32/botha14.html.

Bowman, S. R., Angeli, G., Potts, C., & Manning, C. D. (2015). A large annotated corpus for learning natural language inference. In *Proceedings of EMNLP* (pp. 632–642).

Bowman, S. R., & Dahl, G. (2021). What will it take to fix benchmarking in natural language understanding? In *Proceedings of NAACL*. ACL.

Brown, T., Mann, B., Ryder, N., et al. (2020). Language models are few-shot learners. In H. Larochelle, M. Ranzato, R. Hadsell, et al., eds., *Advances in neural information processing systems* (Vol. 33, pp. 1877–1901). Curran

Associates, Inc. https://proceedings.neurips.cc/paper/2020/file/1457c0d6bf cb4967418bfb8ac142f64a-Paper.pdf.

Burgess, C., & Lund, K. (1995). Hyperspace analogue to language (HAL): A general model of semantic memory. In *Annual meeting of the psychonomic society.*

Bylinina, L., & Tikhonov, A. (2022). The driving forces of polarity-sensitivity: Experiments with multilingual pre-trained neural language models. In *Proceedings of COGSCI* (Vol. 44).

Cer, D., Yang, Y., Kong, S.-Y., et al. (2018). Universal sentence encoder. *arXiv:1803.11175.*

Chaabouni, R., Dessì, R., & Kharitonov, E. (2021). Can Transformers jump around right in natural language? Assessing performance transfer from scan. In *Proceedings of blackboxnlp* (pp. 136–148).

Chaabouni, R., Kharitonov, E., Bouchacourt, D., et al. (2020). Compositionality and generalization in emergent languages. *arXiv:2004.09124.*

Chan, S. C., Santoro, A., Lampinen, A. K., et al. (2022). Data distributional properties drive emergent few-shot learning in transformers. *arXiv:2205.05055.*

Chatzikyriakidis, S., Cooper, R., Dobnik, S., & Larsson, S. (2017). An overview of natural language inference data collection: The way forward? In *Proceedings of the computing natural language inference workshop.*

Chen, T., Jiang, Z., Poliak, A., et al. (2020). Uncertain natural language inference. In *Proceedings of ACL.* ACL.

Chen, Z. (2021). Attentive tree-structured network for monotonicity reasoning. In *Proceedings of NALOMA* (pp. 12–21). ACL.

Chen, Z., Gao, Q., & Moss, L. S. (2021). NeuralLog: Natural language inference with joint neural and logical reasoning. In *Proceedings of *SEM.* ACL.

Cho, K., Van Merriënboer, B., Gulcehre, C., et al. (2014). Learning phrase representations using rnn encoder-decoder for statistical machine translation. *arXiv:1406.1078.*

Chowdhery, A., Narang, S., Devlin, J., et al. (2022). Palm: Scaling language modeling with pathways. *arXiv:2204.02311.*

Clark, H. H. (1996). *Using language.* Cambridge University Press.

Clark, P., Tafjord, O., & Richardson, K. (2021). Transformers as soft reasoners over language. In *Proceedings of IJCAI.*

Clark, S., Coecke, B., & Sadrzadeh, M. (2008). A compositional distributional model of meaning. In *Proceedings of the second quantum interaction symposium (qi-2008)* (pp. 133–140).

Condoravdi, C., Crouch, D., de Paiva, V., et al. (2003). Entailment, intensionality and text understanding. In *Proceedings of the HLT-NAACL 2003 workshop on text meaning* (pp. 38–45).

Cooper, R., Crouch, D., Eijck, J. V., et al. (1996). *Fracas: A framework for computational semantics.* Deliverable D16.

Coppock, E., & Champollion, L. (2022). Invitation to formal semantics. Manuscript, Boston University and New York University.

Dagan, I., Glickman, O., & Magnini, B. (2006). The Pascal recognising textual entailment challenge. In *Proceedings of the Pascal challenges workshop on recognising textual entailment* (pp. 177–190). Springer.

Dagan, I., Roth, D., Sammons, M., & Zanzotto, F. M. (2013). *Recognizing textual entailment: Models and applications.* Morgan & Claypool.

Dalvi, B., Jansen, P., Tafjord, O., et al. (2021). Explaining answers with entailment trees. In *Proceedings of EMNLP* (pp. 7358–7370). ACL.

Dankers, V., Bruni, E., & Hupkes, D. (2022). The paradox of the compositionality of natural language: A neural machine translation case study. In *Proceedings of ACL* (pp. 4154–4175). ACL.

Davis, F. (2022). On the limitations of data: Mismatches between neural models of language and humans (Unpublished doctoral dissertation). Cornell University.

de Deyne, S., Navarro, D. J., Collell, G., & Perfors, A. (2021). Visual and affective multimodal models of word meaning in language and mind. *Cognitive Science, 45*(1). 1–44. https://onlinelibrary.wiley.com/doi/epdf/10.1111/cogs.12922.

de Marneffe, M.-C., Rafferty, A. N., & Manning, C. D. (2008). Finding contradictions in text. In *Proceedings of ACL* (pp. 1039–1047). ACL.

de Marneffe, M.-C., Simons, M., & Tonhauser, J. (2019). The commitmentbank: Investigating projection in naturally occurring discourse. *Proceedings of Sinn und Bedeutung, 23*(2), 107–124.

Devlin, J., Chang, M.-W., Lee, K., & Toutanova, K. (2019). BERT: Pre-training of deep bidirectional transformers for language understanding. In J. Burstein, C. Doran, & T. Solorio, eds., *Proceedings of the 2019 conference of the North American chapter of the association for computational linguistics: Human language technologies, volume 1 (long and short papers)* (pp. 4171–4186). Association for Computational Linguistics. https://aclanthology.org/N19-1423. https://doi.org/10.18653/v1/N19-1423.

Dima, C., de Kok, D., Witte, N., & Hinrichs, E. (2019). No word is an island: A transformation weighting model for semantic composition. *Transactions of the Association for Computational Linguistics, 7*, 437–451.

Drozdov, A., Schärli, N., Akyuürek, E., et al. (2022). Compositional semantic parsing with large language models. *arXiv:2209.15003*.

Du, L., Ding, X., Xiong, K., Liu, T., & Qin, B. (2022). Enhancing pretrained language models with structured commonsense knowledge for textual inference. *Knowledge-Based Systems*, 109488.

Du, Y., Li, S., & Mordatch, I. (2020). Compositional visual generation with energy based models. In *Neurips* (Vol. 33, pp. 6637–6647). Curran Associates, Inc.

Elman, J. L. (1990). Finding structure in time. *Cognitive Science, 14*(2), 179–211.

Ettinger, A. (2020). What BERT is not: Lessons from a new suite of psycholinguistic diagnostics for language models. *Transactions of the Association for Computational Linguistics, 8*, 34–48.

Ettinger, A., Elgohary, A., Phillips, C., & Resnik, P. (2018). Assessing composition in sentence vector representations. In *Proceedings of Coling* (pp. 1790–1801). ACL.

Fitch, F. B. (1973). Natural deduction rules for English. *Philosophical Studies, 24*(2), 89–104.

Frank, S., Bugliarello, E., & Elliott, D. (2021). Vision-and-language or vision-for-language? On cross-modal influence in multimodal transformers. In *Proceedings of EMNLP* (pp. 9847–9857). Association for Computational Linguistics.

Gal, R., Alaluf, Y., Atzmon, Y., Patashnik, O., Bermano, A. H., Chechik, G., & Cohen-Or, D. (2022). *An image is worth one word: Personalizing text-to-image generation using textual inversion.* arXiv.

Gamallo, P. (2021). Compositional distributional semantics with syntactic dependencies and selectional preferences. *Applied Sciences, 11*(12), 1–13.

Gardenfors, P. (2004). Conceptual spaces as a framework for knowledge representation. *Mind and Matter, 2*(2), 9–27.

Gatti, D., Marelli, M., Vecchi, T., & Rinaldi, L. (2022). Spatial representations without spatial computations. *Psychological Science*, 33(11), 1947–1958. https://doi.org/10.1177/09567976221094863.

Geiger, A., Cases, I., Karttunen, L., & Potts, C. (2018). *Stress-testing neural models of natural language inference with multiply-quantified sentences.* arXiv.

Geiger, A., Richardson, K., & Potts, C. (2020). Neural natural language inference models partially embed theories of lexical entailment and negation. In *Proceedings of blackboxnlp* (pp. 163–173).

Giampiccolo, D., Magnini, B., Dagan, I., & Dolan, B. (2007). The third PASCAL recognizing textual entailment challenge. In *Proceedings of the ACL-PASCAL workshop on textual entailment and paraphrasing*. ACL.

Gleitman, L. (1990). The structural sources of verb meanings. *Language Acquisition, 1*(1), 3–55.

Gleitman, L. R., Cassidy, K., Nappa, R., Papafragou, A., & Trueswell, J. C. (2005). Hard words. *Language Learning and Development, 1*(1), 23–64.

Goyal, Y., Khot, T., Summers-Stay, D., Batra, D., & Parikh, D. (2017). Making the v in vqa matter: Elevating the role of image understanding in visual question answering. In *Proceedings of IEEE/CVF CVPR* (pp. 6904–6913).

Greenberg, G. (2013). Beyond resemblance. *Philosophical Review, 122*(2).

Greenberg, G. (2021). Semantics of pictorial space. *Review of Philosophy and Psychology, 12*(4), 847–887.

Grefenstette, E., Dinu, G., Zhang, Y.- Z., et al. (2013). Multi-step regression learning for compositional distributional semantics. *arXiv:1301.6939*.

Guevara, E. R. (2011). Computing semantic compositionality in distributional semantics. In *Proceedings of the ninth international conference on computational semantics* (pp. 135–144).

Gururangan, S., Swayamdipta, S., Levy, O., et al. (2018). Annotation artifacts in natural language inference data. In *Proceedings of NAACL* (pp. 107–112). ACL.

Guu, K., Lee, K., Tung, Z., et al. (2020). *Realm: Retrieval-augmented language model pre-training*. arXiv.

Hacquard, V., & Lidz, J. (2022). On the acquisition of attitude verbs. *Annual Review of Linguistics, 8*, 193–212.

Harnad, S. (1990). The symbol grounding problem. *Physica D: Nonlinear Phenomena, 42*(1–3), 335–346.

Harris, R. A. (1993). *The linguistics wars*. Oxford University Press on Demand.

Hartmann, M., de Lhoneux, M., Hershcovich, D., et al. (2021). A multilingual benchmark for probing negation-awareness with minimal pairs. In *Proceedings of CONLL* (pp. 244–257). ACL.

Hawthorne, C., Jaegle, A., Cangea, C., et al. (2022). General-purpose, long-context autoregressive modeling with perceiver ar. *arXiv:2202.07765*.

He, Q., Wang, H., & Zhang, Y. (2020). Enhancing generalization in natural language inference by syntax. In *Findings of EMNLP*. ACL.

Hessel, J., & Lee, L. (2020). Does my multimodal model learn cross-modal interactions? It's harder to tell than you might think! In *Proceedings of EMNLP* (pp. 861–877).

Hill, F., Cho, K., & Korhonen, A. (2016). Learning distributed representations of sentences from unlabelled data. In *Proceedings of NAACL* (pp. 1367–1377).

Hochreiter, S., & Schmidhuber, J. (1997). Long short-term memory. *Neural Computation, 9*(8), 1735–1780.

Hofmann, V., Pierrehumbert, J. B., & Schütze, H. (2021). Superbizarre is not superb: Derivational morphology improves BERT's interpretation of complex words. *arXiv:2101.00403*.

Hong, R., Liu, D., Mo, X., et al. (2019). Learning to compose and reason with language tree structures for visual grounding. *IEEE transactions on pattern analysis and machine intelligence*.

Hossain, M. M., Kovatchev, V., Dutta, P., et al. (2020). An analysis of natural language inference benchmarks through the lens of negation. In *Proceedings of EMNLP* (pp. 9106–9118). ACL.

Hu, H., Chen, Q., & Moss, L. (2019). Natural language inference with monotonicity. In *Proceedings of IWCS* (pp. 8–15). ACL.

Hudson, D. A., & Manning, C. D. (2018). Compositional attention networks for machine reasoning. In *International Conference on Learning Representations*.

Hudson, D. A., & Manning, C. D. (2019). Gqa: A new dataset for real-world visual reasoning and compositional question answering. In *Proceedings of IEEE/CVF CVPR* (pp. 6700–6709).

Hupkes, D., Dankers, V., Mul, M., & Bruni, E. (2020). Compositionality decomposed: How do neural networks generalise? *Journal of Artificial Intelligence Research, 67*, 757–795.

Hupkes, D., Giulianelli, M., Dankers, V., et al. (2022). *State-of-the-art generalisation research in NLP: A taxonomy and review*.

Hupkes, D., Veldhoen, S., & Zuidema, W. (2018). Visualisation and "diagnostic classifiers" reveal how recurrent and recursive neural networks process hierarchical structure. *Journal of Artificial Intelligence Research, 61*(1), 907–926.

Icard, T. F. (2012). Inclusion and exclusion in natural language. *Studia Logica, 100*(4), 705–725.

Icard, T. F., & Moss, L. S. (2014). Recent progress on monotonicity. *LILT, 9*.

Irsoy, O., & Cardie, C. (2014). Deep recursive neural networks for compositionality in language. *NeurIPS, 27*, 1–9.

Jeretic, P., Warstadt, A., Bhooshan, S., & Williams, A. (2020). Are natural language inference models IMPPRESsive? Learning IMPlicature and PRESupposition. In *Proceedings of ACL* (pp. 8690–8705). ACL.

Jiang, N., & de Marneffe, M.-C. (2019). Evaluating BERT for natural language inference: A case study on the CommitmentBank. In *Proceedings of EMNLP–IJCNLP* (pp. 6086–6091). ACL.

Jinman, Z., Zhong, S., Zhang, X., & Liang, Y. (2020). Pbos: Probabilistic bag-of-subwords for generalizing word embedding. *arXiv:2010.10813*.

Johnson, J., Hariharan, B., Van der Maaten, L., et al. (2017). Clevr: A diagnostic dataset for compositional language and elementary visual reasoning. In *Proceedings of IEEE/CVF CVPR* (pp. 2901–2910).

Jumelet, J., Denic, M., Szymanik, J., et al. (2021). Language models use monotonicity to assess NPI licensing. In *Findings of ACL–IJCNLP* (pp. 4958–4969). ACL.

Kalouli, A.-L., Hu, H., Webb, A. F., et al. (2023). Curing the SICK and other NLI maladies. *Computational Linguistics*, *49*(1), 199–243.

Kalouli, A.-L., Real, L., & de Paiva, V. (2017). Textual inference: Getting logic from humans. In *Proceedings of IWCS*.

Kartsaklis, D., Sadrzadeh, M., & Pulman, S. (2013). Separating disambiguation from composition in distributional semantics. In *Proceedings of CONLL* (pp. 114–123). ACL.

Kassner, N., & Schütze, H. (2020). Negated and misprimed probes for pretrained language models: Birds can talk, but cannot fly. In *Proceedings of ACL* (pp. 7811–7818). ACL.

Khan, S., Naseer, M., Hayat, M., et al. (2021). Transformers in vision: A survey. *ACM computing surveys (CSUR)*.

Kiela, D., Bulat, L., & Clark, S. (2015). Grounding semantics in olfactory perception. In *Proceedings of ACL* (pp. 231–236).

Kim, N., & Linzen, T. (2020). Cogs: A compositional generalization challenge based on semantic interpretation. In *Proceedings of EMNLP*.

Kim, N., & Schuster, S. (2023). Entity tracking in language models. In *Proceedings of ACL* (pp. 3835–3855). ACL.

Kirby, S., Cornish, H., & Smith, K. (2008). Cumulative cultural evolution in the laboratory: An experimental approach to the origins of structure in human language. *Proceedings of the National Academy of Sciences*, *105*(31), 10681–10686.

Kirby, S., Tamariz, M., Cornish, H., & Smith, K. (2015). Compression and communication in the cultural evolution of linguistic structure. *Cognition*, *141*, 87–102.

Kober, T., Bijl de Vroe, S., & Steedman, M. (2019). Temporal and aspectual entailment. In *Proceedings of IWCS* (pp. 103–119). ACL.

Kracht, M. (2011). *Interpreted languages and compositionality* (Vol. 89). Springer Science & Business Media.

Kratzer, A., & Heim, I. (1998). *Semantics in generative grammar* (Vol. 1185). Blackwell Oxford.

Krishna, R., Zhu, Y., Groth, O., et al. (2017). Visual genome: Connecting language and vision using crowdsourced dense image annotations. *International Journal of Computer Vision, 123*(1), 32–73.

Kudo, T., & Richardson, J. (2018). *Sentencepiece: A simple and language independent subword tokenizer and detokenizer for neural text processing.*

Lai, A., & Hockenmaier, J. (2014). Illinois-LH: A denotational and distributional approach to semantics. In *Proceedings of SemEval* (pp. 329–334). ACL.

Lake, B., & Baroni, M. (2018). Generalization without systematicity: On the compositional skills of sequence-to-sequence recurrent networks. In *ICML*.

Lakoff, G. (1970). Linguistics and natural logic. *Synthese, 22*(1), 151–271.

Landau, B., & Gleitman, L. R. (1985). *Language and experience: Evidence from the blind child.* Harvard University Press.

Landauer, T. K., & Dumais, S. T. (1997). A solution to Plato's problem: The latent semantic analysis theory of acquisition, induction, and representation of knowledge. *Psychological Review, 104*(2), 211–240.

Lazaridou, A., Marelli, M., Zamparelli, R., & Baroni, M. (2013). Compositional-ly derived representations of morphologically complex words in distributional semantics. In *Proceedings of ACL* (pp. 1517–1526).

Le, P., & Zuidema, W. (2015). Compositional distributional semantics with long short term memory. *arXiv:1503.02510.*

Levy, O., & Goldberg, Y. (2014). Neural word embedding as implicit matrix factorization. *NeurIPS, 27,* 1–9.

Lewis, D. (1970). General semantics. *Synthese, 22*(1/2), 18–67.

Li, B. Z., Nye, M., & Andreas, J. (2021). Implicit representations of meaning in neural language models. *arXiv:2106.00737.*

Li, F., Zhang, H., Zhang, Y.-F., et al. (2022). Vision-language intelligence: Tasks, representation learning, and large models. *arXiv:2203.01922.*

Li, L. H., Yatskar, M., Yin, D., et al. (2019). Visualbert: A simple and performant baseline for vision and language. *arXiv:1908.03557.*

Lin, T.-Y., Maire, M., Belongie, S., et al. (2014). Microsoft Coco: Common objects in context. In *European conference on computer vision* (pp. 740–755).

Lin, Z., Feng, M., dos Santos, C. N., et al. (2017). A structured self-attentive sentence embedding. In *ICLR*.

Linzen, T., & Baroni, M. (2021). Syntactic structure from deep learning. *Annual Review of Linguistics, 7,* 195–212.

Liu, A., Wu, Z., Michael, J., et al. (2023). We're afraid language models aren't modeling ambiguity. In H. Bouamor, J. Pino, & K. Bali, eds., *Proceedings of the 2023 conference on empirical methods in natural language processing* (pp. 790–807). Association for Computational Linguistics. https://aclanthology.org/2023.emnlp-main.51. https://doi.org/10.18653/v1/2023.emnlp-main.51.

Liu, Y., Ott, M., Goyal, N., et al. (2019). Roberta: A robustly optimized BERT pretraining approach. *arXiv:1907.11692*.

Lu, J., Batra, D., Parikh, D., & Lee, S. (2019). Vilbert: Pretraining task-agnostic visiolinguistic representations for vision-and-language tasks. *NeurIPS*.

Lu, J., Goswami, V., Rohrbach, M., et al. (2020). 12-in-1: Multi-task vision and language representation learning. In *Proceedings of IEEE/CVF CVPR* (pp. 10437–10446).

Luong, M.-T., Socher, R., & Manning, C. D. (2013). Better word representations with recursive neural networks for morphology. In *Proceedings of CONLL*.

MacCartney, B., & Manning, C. D. (2007). Natural logic for textual inference. In *Proceedings of the ACL-PASCAL workshop on textual entailment and paraphrasing* (pp. 193–200). ACL.

MacCartney, B., & Manning, C. D. (2009). An extended model of natural logic. In *Proceedings of IWCS* (pp. 140–156). ACL.

Mao, J., Huang, J., Toshev, A., et al. (2016). Generation and comprehension of unambiguous object descriptions. In *Proceedings of IEEE/CVF CVPR* (pp. 11–20).

Marelli, M., Menini, S., Baroni, M., et al. (2014). A sick cure for the evaluation of compositional distributional semantic models. In *Proceedings of LREC* (pp. 216–223).

Margolis, E. E., & Laurence, S. E. (1999). *Concepts: Core readings.* MIT Press.

McCoy, R. T., Linzen, T., Dunbar, E., & Smolensky, P. (2019). RNNs implicitly implement tensor-product representations. In *ICLR*.

McCoy, R. T., Pavlick, E., & Linzen, T. (2019). Right for the wrong reasons: Diagnosing syntactic heuristics in natural language inference. In *Proceedings of ACL* (pp. 3428–3448). ACL.

Merrill, W., Warstadt, A., & Linzen, T. (2022). *Entailment semantics can be extracted from an ideal language model.* arXiv.

Merullo, J., Eickhoff, C., & Pavlick, E. (2023). *A mechanism for solving relational tasks in transformer language models.*

Meteyard, L., Cuadrado, S. R., Bahrami, B., & Vigliocco, G. (2012). Coming of age: A review of embodiment and the neuroscience of semantics. *Cortex*, *48*(7), 788–804.

Mickus, T., Bernard, T., & Paperno, D. (2020). What meaning–form correlation has to compose with: A study of MFC on artificial and natural language. In *Proceedings of COLING* (pp. 3737–3749). International Committee on Computational Linguistics.

Mickus, T., Paperno, D., & Constant, M. (2022). How to dissect a Muppet: The structure of transformer embedding spaces. *TACL, 10*, 981–996.

Mikolov, T., Chen, K., Corrado, G., & Dean, J. (2013). Efficient estimation of word representations in vector space. *arXiv:1301.3781*.

Mitchell, J., & Lapata, M. (2010). Composition in distributional models of semantics. *Cognitive Science, 34*(8), 1388–1429.

Montague, R. (1970). English as a formal language. In *Linguaggi nella societa e nella tecnica* (pp. 188–221). Edizioni di Communita.

Montague, R. (1973). The proper treatment of quantification in ordinary English. In *Approaches to natural language* (pp. 221–242). Springer.

Moss, L. S. (2010). Natural logic and semantics. In *Logic, language and meaning* (pp. 84–93). Springer.

Moss, L. S. (2015). Natural logic. *The handbook of contemporary semantic theory* (pp. 559–592).

Murzi, J., & Steinberger, F. (2017). Inferentialism. *A Companion to the Philosophy of Language, 1*, 197–224.

Naik, A., Ravichander, A., Sadeh, N., et al. (2018). Stress test evaluation for natural language inference. In *Proceedings of COLING* (pp. 2340–2353). ACL.

Nangia, N., & Bowman, S. (2018). ListOps: A diagnostic dataset for latent tree learning. In *Proceedings of NAACL: Student research workshop*. ACL.

Nie, Y., Zhou, X., & Bansal, M. (2020). What can we learn from collective human opinions on natural language inference data? In *Proceedings of EMNLP* (pp. 9131–9143). ACL.

Nivre, J., de Marneffe, M.-C., Ginter, F., et al. (2020). Universal Dependencies v2: An evergrowing multilingual treebank collection. In *Proceedings of LREC*. ELRA.

Nye, M., Solar-Lezama, A., Tenenbaum, J., & Lake, B. M. (2020). Learning compositional rules via neural program synthesis. *NeurIPS, 33*, 10832–10842.

Olsson, C., Elhage, N., Nanda, N., et al. (2022). In-context learning and induction heads. *arXiv:2209.11895*.

Ouyang, L., Wu, J., Jiang, X., et al. (2022). Training language models to follow instructions with human feedback. *NeurIPS, 35*, 27730–27744.

Paperno, D. (2022). On learning interpreted languages wit–h recurrent models. *Computational Linguistics, 48*(2), 471–482.

Paperno, D., & Baroni, M. (2016). When the whole is less than the sum of its parts: How composition affects pmi values in distributional semantic vectors. *Computational Linguistics, 42*(2), 345–350.

Paperno, D., Kruszewski, G., Lazaridou, A., et al. (2016). The LAMBADA dataset: Word prediction requiring a broad discourse context. In *Proceedings of ACL.*

Paperno, D., Pham, N. T., & Baroni, M. (2014). A practical and linguistically-motivated approach to compositional distributional semantics. In *Proceedings of ACL* (pp. 90–99). ACL.

Parcalabescu, L., Cafagna, M., Muradjan, L., et al. (2022). Valse: A task-independent benchmark for vision and language models centered on linguistic phenomena. In *Proceedings of ACL.*

Parcalabescu, L., & Frank, A. (2022). Mm-shap: A performance-agnostic metric for measuring multimodal contributions in vision and language models & tasks. *arXiv:2212.08158.*

Parikh, P. (2001). *The use of language.* CSLI Publications.

Parrish, A., Schuster, S., Warstadt, A., et al. (2021). NOPE: A corpus of naturally-occurring presuppositions in English. In *Proceedings of CONLL* (pp. 349–366). ACL.

Patel, A., Li, B., Rasooli, M. S., et al. (2022). Bidirectional language models are also few-shot learners. *arXiv:2209.14500.*

Pavlick, E., & Kwiatkowski, T. (2019). Inherent disagreements in human textual inferences. *TACL, 7,* 677–694.

Pennington, J., Socher, R., & Manning, C. D. (2014). Glove: Global vectors for word representation. In *Proceedings of EMNLP* (pp. 1532–1543).

Pérez, J., Barceló, P., & Marinkovic, J. (2021). Attention is Turing complete. *Journal of Machine Learning Research, 22*(1), 3463–3497.

Pezzelle, S. (2023). Dealing with semantic underspecification in multimodal NLP. In *Proceedings of ACL* (pp. 12098–12112). ACL.

Pezzelle, S., Takmaz, E., & Fernández, R. (2021). Word representation learning in multimodal pre-trained transformers: An intrinsic evaluation. *TACL, 9,* 1563–1579.

Piantadosi, S. T., & Hill, F. (2022). *Meaning without reference in large language models.* arXiv.

Pinter, Y., Guthrie, R., & Eisenstein, J. (2017). Mimicking word embeddings using subword rnns. *arXiv:1707.06961.*

Poliak, A. (2020). A survey on recognizing textual entailment as an NLP evaluation. In *Proceedings of the first workshop on evaluation and comparison of NLP systems* (pp. 92–109). ACL.

Poliak, A., Haldar, A., Rudinger, R., et al. (2018). Collecting diverse natural language inference problems for sentence representation evaluation. In *Proceedings of EMNLP* (pp. 67–81). ACL.

Poliak, A., Naradowsky, J., Haldar, A., et al. (2018). Hypothesis only baselines in natural language inference. In *Proceedings of *SEM* (pp. 180–191). ACL.

Potts, C. (2020). *Is it possible for language models to achieve language understanding?* (Medium post).

Prokhorov, V., Pilehvar, M. T., Kartsaklis, D., et al. (2019). Unseen word representation by aligning heterogeneous lexical semantic spaces. In *Proceedings of the AAAI conference on artificial intelligence* (Vol. 33, pp. 6900–6907).

Pullum, G. K., & Huddleston, R. (2002). Negation. In *The Cambridge grammar of the English language* (pp. 785–850). Cambridge University Press.

Radford, A., Kim, J. W., Hallacy, C., et al. (2021). Learning transferable visual models from natural language supervision. In *ICML* (pp. 8748–8763).

Radford, A., Wu, J., Child, R., et al. (2019). Language models are unsupervised multitask learners.

Rajaee, S., Yaghoobzadeh, Y., & Pilehvar, M. T. (2022). Looking at the overlooked: An analysis on the word-overlap bias in natural language inference. In *Proceedings of EMNLP* (pp. 10605–10616). ACL.

Rajpurkar, P., Zhang, J., Lopyrev, K., & Liang, P. (2016). Squad: 100,000+ questions for machine comprehension of text. *arXiv:1606.05250*.

Ramesh, A., Dhariwal, P., Nichol, A., et al. (2022). *Hierarchical text-conditional image generation with clip latents.* arXiv.

Rassin, R., Ravfogel, S., & Goldberg, Y. (2022). Dalle-2 is seeing double: Flaws in word-to-concept mapping in text2image models. *arXiv:2210.10606*.

Ravichander, A., Naik, A., Rose, C., & Hovy, E. (2019). EQUATE: A benchmark evaluation framework for quantitative reasoning in natural language inference. In *Proceedings of CONLL* (pp. 349–361). ACL.

Ribeiro, M. T., Wu, T., Guestrin, C., & Singh, S. (2020). Beyond accuracy: Behavioral testing of NLP models with CheckList. In *Proceedings of ACL* (pp. 4902–4912). ACL.

Richardson, K., Hu, H., Moss, L. S., & Sabharwal, A. (2020). Probing natural language inference models through semantic fragments. In *AAAI*.

Ritter, S., Long, C., Paperno, D., et al. (2015). Leveraging preposition ambiguity to assess compositional distributional models of semantics. In *Proceedings of *SEM*.

Rogers, A., Kovaleva, O., & Rumshisky, A. (2020). A primer in BERTology: What we know about how BERT works. *TACL, 8*, 842–866.

Rogers, A., & Rumshisky, A. (2020). A guide to the dataset explosion in QA, NLI, and commonsense reasoning. In *Proceedings of COLING: Tutorial abstracts* (pp. 27–32). International Committee for Computational Linguistics.

Rombach, R., Blattmann, A., Lorenz, D., et al. (2021). *High-resolution image synthesis with latent diffusion models.*

Ross, A., & Pavlick, E. (2019). How well do NLI models capture verb veridicality? In *Proceedings of EMNLP–IJCNLP* (pp. 2230–2240). ACL.

Ruiz, N., Li, Y., Jampani, V., et al. (2022). *Dreambooth: Fine tuning text-to-image diffusion models for subject-driven generation.* arXiv.

Ryzhova, D., Kyuseva, M., & Paperno, D. (2016). Typology of adjectives benchmark for compositional distributional models. In *Proceedings of LREC* (pp. 1253–1257).

Saha, S., Ghosh, S., Srivastava, S., & Bansal, M. (2020). PRover: Proof generation for interpretable reasoning over rules. In *Proceedings of EMNLP* (pp. 122–136). ACL.

Saha, S., Nie, Y., & Bansal, M. (2020). ConjNLI: Natural language inference over conjunctive sentences. In *Proceedings of EMNLP.* ACL.

Saharia, C., Chan, W., Saxena, S., et al. (2022). Photorealistic text-to-image diffusion models with deep language understanding. *Advances in Neural Information Processing Systems*, *35*, 36479–36494.

Schlag, I., Smolensky, P., Fernandez, R., et al. (2019). Enhancing the transformer with explicit relational encoding for math problem solving. *arXiv:1910.06611.*

Schlenker, P. (2018). What is super semantics? *Philosophical Perspectives*, *32*(1), 365–453.

Schroeder-Heister, P. (2018). Proof-theoretic semantics. In *The Stanford encyclopedia of philosophy* (Spring 2018 ed.). Metaphysics Research Lab, Stanford University.

Schuster, S., Chen, Y., & Degen, J. (2020). Harnessing the linguistic signal to predict scalar inferences. In *Proceedings of ACL* (pp. 5387–5403). ACL.

Sennrich, R., Haddow, B., & Birch, A. (2015). Neural machine translation of rare words with subword units. *arXiv:1508.07909.*

Smolensky, P. (1990). Tensor product variable binding and the representation of symbolic structures in connectionist systems. *Artificial Intelligence*, *46*(1–2), 159–216.

Socher, R., Huval, B., Manning, C. D., & Ng, A. Y. (2012). Semantic compositionality through recursive matrix-vector spaces. In *Proceedings of EMNLP–CONLL* (pp. 1201–1211).

Socher, R., Perelygin, A., Wu, J., et al. (2013). Recursive deep models for semantic compositionality over a sentiment treebank. In *Proceedings of EMNLP* (pp. 1631–1642).

Sommers, F. (1982). *The logic of natural language.* Oxford University Press.

Song, X., Salcianu, A., Song, Y., et al. (2021). Fast WordPiece tokenization. In *Proceedings of EMNLP.* ACL.

Soricut, R., & Och, F. J. (2015). Unsupervised morphology induction using word embeddings. In *Proceedings of NAACL* (pp. 1627–1637).

Soulos, P., McCoy, R. T., Linzen, T., & Smolensky, P. (2020). Discovering the compositional structure of vector representations with role learning networks. In *Proceedings of blackboxnlp* (pp. 238–254). ACL.

Srivastava, A., Rastogi, A., Rao, A., et al. (2022). Beyond the imitation game: Quantifying and extrapolating the capabilities of language models. *arXiv:2206.04615.*

Storks, S., Gao, Q., & Chai, J. Y. (2019). *Recent advances in natural language inference: A survey of benchmarks, resources, and approaches.* arXiv.

Suhr, A., Lewis, M., Yeh, J., & Artzi, Y. (2017). A corpus of natural language for visual reasoning. In *Proceedings of ACL* (pp. 217–223).

Tafjord, O., Dalvi, B., & Clark, P. (2021). ProofWriter: Generating implications, proofs, and abductive statements over natural language. In *Findings of ACL–IJCNLP* (pp. 3621–3634). ACL.

Tan, H., & Bansal, M. (2019). Lxmert: Learning cross-modality encoder representations from transformers. *arXiv:1908.07490.*

Tan, H., & Bansal, M. (2020). Vokenization: Improving language understanding with contextualized, visual-grounded supervision. *arXiv:2010.06775.*

Thrush, T., Jiang, R., Bartolo, M., et al. (2022). Winoground: Probing vision and language models for visio-linguistic compositionality. In *Proceedings of IEEE/CVF CVPR.*

Tikhonov, A., Bylinina, L., & Paperno, D. (2023). Leverage points in modality shifts: Comparing language-only and multimodal word representations. In *Proceedings of *SEM* (pp. 11–17). ACL.

Tokmakov, P., Wang, Y.-X., & Hebert, M. (2019). Learning compositional representations for few-shot recognition. In *Proceedings of IEEE/CVF ICCV* (pp. 6372–6381).

Touvron, H., Martin, L., Stone, K., et al. (2023). Llama 2: Open foundation and fine-tuned chat models. *arXiv:2307.09288.*

Truong, T., Baldwin, T., Cohn, T., & Verspoor, K. (2022). Improving negation detection with negation-focused pre-training. In *Proceedings of NAACL* (pp. 4188–4193). ACL.

Truong, T. H., Otmakhova, Y., Baldwin, T., et al. (2022). Not another negation benchmark: The NaN–NLI test suite for sub-clausal negation. In *Proceedings of AACL–IJCNLP* (pp. 883–894). ACL.

Tsuchiya, M. (2018). Performance impact caused by hidden bias of training data for recognizing textual entailment. In *Proceedings of LREC*. ELRA.

Turing, A. M. (2009). Computing machinery and intelligence. In *Parsing the Turing test* (pp. 23–65). Springer.

Van Benthem, J. (1986). Natural logic. In *Essays in logical semantics* (pp. 109–119). Springer Netherlands.

Van Benthem, J. (2008). A brief history of natural logic. In *Logic, navya-nyaya and applications, homage to Bimal Krishna Matilal.* College Publications.

Vashishtha, S., Poliak, A., Lal, Y. K., et al. (2020). Temporal reasoning in natural language inference. In *Findings of EMNLP* (pp. 4070–4078). ACL.

Vaswani, A., Shazeer, N., Parmar, N., et al. (2017). Attention is all you need. In *Neurips.*

Vedantam, R., Bengio, S., Murphy, K., et al. (2017). Context-aware captions from context-agnostic supervision. In *Proceedings of IEEE/CVF CVPR* (pp. 251–260).

Verga, P., Sun, H., Soares, L. B., & Cohen, W. W. (2020). *Facts as experts: Adaptable and interpretable neural memory over symbolic knowledge.* arXiv.

Vulić, I., Baker, S., Ponti, E. M., et al. (2020). Multi-simlex: A large-scale evaluation of multilingual and crosslingual lexical semantic similarity. *Computational Linguistics*, *46*(4), 847–897.

Wang, A., Pruksachatkun, Y., Nangia, N., et al. (2019). Superglue: A stickier benchmark for general-purpose language understanding systems. In *Neurips* (Vol. 32). Curran Associates, Inc.

Wang, A., Singh, A., Michael, J., et al. (2019). GLUE: A multi-task benchmark and analysis platform for natural language understanding. In *ICLR.*

Warstadt, A., & Bowman, S. R. (2022). What artificial neural networks can tell us about human language acquisition. *arXiv:2208.07998.*

Weiss, G., Goldberg, Y., & Yahav, E. (2018). On the practical computational power of finite precision rnns for language recognition. In *Proceedings of ACL* (pp. 740–745).

White, A. S., Rastogi, P., Duh, K., & Van Durme, B. (2017). Inference is everything: Recasting semantic resources into a unified evaluation framework. In *Proceedings of IJCNLP* (pp. 996–1005). Asian Federation of Natural Language Processing.

Williams, A., Nangia, N., & Bowman, S. (2018). A broad-coverage challenge corpus for sentence understanding through inference. In *Proceedings of NAACL* (pp. 1112–1122). ACL.

Yanaka, H., Mineshima, K., Bekki, D., & Inui, K. (2020). Do neural models learn systematicity of monotonicity inference in natural language? In *Proceedings of ACL* (pp. 6105–6117). ACL.

Yanaka, H., Mineshima, K., Bekki, D., et al. (2019a). Can neural networks understand monotonicity reasoning? In *Proceedings of blackboxnlp* (pp. 31–40).

Yanaka, H., Mineshima, K., Bekki, D., et al. (2019b). HELP: A dataset for identifying shortcomings of neural models in monotonicity reasoning. In *Proceedings of *SEM*.

Yang, Z., Dai, Z., Yang, Y., et al. (2019). Xlnet: Generalized autoregressive pretraining for language understanding. In *Neurips* (Vol. 32). Curran Associates, Inc.

Yi, K., Gan, C., Li, Y., et al. (2019). Clevrer: Collision events for video representation and reasoning. *arXiv:1910.01442*.

Yuksekgonul, M., Bianchi, F., Kalluri, P., et al. (2022). *When and why vision-language models behave like bags-of-words, and what to do about it?* arXiv.

Yun, T., Bhalla, U., Pavlick, E., & Sun, C. (2022). Do vision-language pretrained models learn primitive concepts? *arXiv:2203.17271*.

Zaenen, A., Karttunen, L., & Crouch, R. (2005). Local textual inference: Can it be defined or circumscribed? In *Proceedings of the ACL workshop on empirical modeling of semantic equivalence and entailment.* ACL.

Zhang, C., Van Durme, B., Li, Z., & Stengel-Eskin, E. (2022). Visual commonsense in pretrained unimodal and multimodal models. *arXiv:2205.01850*.

Zhang, C., Yang, Z., He, X., & Deng, L. (2020). Multimodal intelligence: Representation learning, information fusion, and applications. *IEEE Journal of Selected Topics in Signal Processing, 14*(3), 478–493.

Zhou, D., Schärli, N., Hou, L., et al. (2022). Least-to-most prompting enables complex reasoning in large language models. *arXiv:2205.10625*.

Zhou, Y., Liu, C., & Pan, Y. (2016). Modelling sentence pairs with tree-structured attentive encoder. In *Proceedings of COLING* (pp. 2912–2922). The COLING 2016 Organizing Committee.

Acknowledgments

We would like to thank – in alphabetical order – Albert Gatt, Dmitry Kourmyshov, Emar Maier, Timothee Mickus, Rick Nouwen, and Joost Zwarts for discussions, help with illustrations, and feedback on previous drafts. We would also like to thank anonymous reviewers who read an earlier version of this Element and gave us illuminating feedback. This allowed us to improve the text in many ways. Last but certainly not least we would like to thank Jonathan Ginzburg and Daniel Lassiter, the editors of Cambridge Elements in Semantics, for their patience, comments, and encouragement. Any remaining issues are our own. Part of this work was conducted while Lisa Bylinina held a position at the Center for Language and Cognition, University of Groningen. Lasha Abzianidze was partially supported by the European Research Council (ERC) under the European Union's Horizon 2020 research and innovation programme (grant agreement No 742204).

Cambridge Elements ≡

Semantics

Jonathan Ginzburg
Université Paris-Cité

Jonathan Ginzburg is Professor of Linguistics at Université Paris-Cité (formerly Paris 7). He has held appointments at the Hebrew University of Jerusalem and King's College, London. He is one of the founders and currently associate editor of the journal *Dialogue and Discourse*. His research interests include semantics, dialogue, and language acquisition. He is the author of *Interrogative Investigations* (CSLI Publications, 2001, with Ivan A. Sag) and *The Interactive Stance: Meaning for Conversation* (Oxford University Press, 2012).

Daniel Lassiter
University of Edinburgh

Daniel Lassiter is Senior Lecturer in Semantics in Linguistics & English Language at the University of Edinburgh. He works on topics at the intersection of formal semantics/pragmatics, cognitive psychology, and philosophy of language, including modality, conditionals, vagueness, scalar semantics, and Bayesian pragmatics. He is the author of *Graded Modality* (Oxford University Press, 2017) and numerous journal articles.

About the Series

Elements in Semantics emphasizes the field's recent flourishing of interdisciplinary work, connecting linguistics and philosophy with cognitive science, computer science, neuroscience, law, anthropology, sociology, economics, and beyond. The series should be of interest to a broad community of researchers interested in the study of meaning from diverse perspectives.

Semantics